DATE DUE

THE *PANAY* INCIDENT: PRELUDE TO WAR

THE *PANAY* INCIDENT: PRELUDE TO WAR

(by) MANNY T. KOGINOS

Illustrated

1967
Purdue University Studies
Lafayette, Indiana

To my parents
ANDREW AND KATHERINE KOGINOS
—whose sacrifice made this book possible

PREFACE

The *Panay* incident in retrospect was the most dramatic single event in Japanese-American relations during the 1930's. The attack upon the American gunboat by Japanese forces in December, 1937, contributed greatly to the general deterioration and eventual breakdown in American-Japanese diplomatic relations. Though the immediate impact of the incident did not result in any radical departure from America's isolationist position, it did modify American opinion in respect to foreign and domestic affairs. Indeed, pacifist influence was to reach its highest crest during the *Panay* episode. At the same time, the crisis dramatized vividly America's unwillingness to pursue a more positive policy in the Far East. The incident, however, did point out the need for military preparedness, and in the end, the affair served as one of the essential driving forces behind an upward surge of navalism which occurred in the spring of 1938.

This study is concerned with the events preceding the sinking of the *Panay* and the immediate issues which followed. Chapter I briefly describes American policy in the Far East during the inter-war period and reviews American attempts to protect its nationals and interests in China following the outbreak of hostilities between China and Japan in July, 1937. It also examines the Japanese attitude toward non-belligerents in the war zone. Chapter II deals in detail with the bombing and sinking of the *Panay* and reviews the domestic and foreign attitudes toward the episode. Chapter III analyzes the diplomatic implications involved in the crisis, the reaction of the Roosevelt Administration and the final settlement of the affair. It also includes the reaction of the British and other European governments to the incident. Chapter IV reviews the Ludlow Referendum on war, its potential effect upon future diplomacy and the public response to the resolution. Chapter V analyzes the causes for naval expansion, the foreign and domestic editorial reaction to Roosevelt's naval program and the Congressional debate which ensued on the issue. The final chapter briefly reviews and analyzes the causes of the *Panay* sinking and the events immediately following.

I would like to extend my sincere appreciation and thanks to Dr. Dorothy D. Gondos, the late Dr. E. Taylor Parks and Dr. Walter Rundell. I particularly wish to express my gratitude to Dr. Arthur A. Ekirch, Jr. whose advice, assistance, and encouragement had been invaluable in the completion of this book.

Manny T. Koginos

West Lafayette, Indiana

TABLE OF CONTENTS

INTRODUCTION

American foreign policy traditionally sought to maintain the status quo in the Far East and to uphold the territorial integrity of China; at the same time, the United States attempted to avoid any alliances with other powers in Far Eastern affairs. As early as 1900 when Secretary of State John Hay first proposed his open-door policy in regard to China, Japan, in particular, challenged American efforts by endeavoring to extend its influence on the Chinese mainland and in Siberia.* Tension continued to mount following the First World War and the United States government called upon the major powers of the world to meet in Washington in the hope that some understanding or agreement could be reached to preserve the status quo in the Far East. Though the Washington Conference focused its attention upon ending the three-cornered naval rivalry between the United States, Great Britain, and Japan, delegates at the meeting, nevertheless, signed an agreement on February 6, 1922, which in essence endorsed the American policy of the open door. More importantly, the signatories from the United States, Great Britain, Japan, France, Italy, Portugal, Belgium, and the Netherlands agreed "to respect the sovereignty, the independence and the territorial and administrative integrity of China." In other words, the so-called Nine Power Treaty expressly prohibited the establishment of spheres of influence in that country.[1]

Prior to signing the Nine Power Treaty, Secretary of State Charles Evans Hughes, the American representative to the conference, attempted to find some substitute which would terminate the Anglo-Japanese alliance of 1902. The alliance had been formulated originally as a defensive measure against a possible threat from Germany and Russia but these powers had ceased to be obstacles to Japan and Hughes believed that the agreement was now aimed

---

* Hay's open-door policy was a measure by which he sought to secure for the United States equal trading privileges within the spheres of interest which the major powers had established in China.

1

at the United States. To alleviate this problem, the United States, Great Britain, Japan, and France signed the so-called Four Power Pact on December 13, 1921 which abrogated the Anglo-Japanese alliance. Under its provisions, the four powers also agreed "to respect their rights in relation to their insular possessions and insular dominions in the region of the Pacific." For the United States, the Four Power Pact and the Nine Power Treaty had a triple value; they ended the Anglo-Japanese alliance, they reaffirmed Japan's promise to respect American sovereignty in the Philippines, and they served as a check to further Japanese expansion in the Far East.[2]

In 1931, however, Japan openly defied the agreements reached at the Washington Conference by launching a war of conquest and pacification of Manchuria. This challenge did not go unopposed and within the next two years the United States refused to recognize any changes which Japan was forcing on the mainland of Asia. Indeed, the Sino-Japanese conflict over Manchuria ran counter to the Administration's inclination that it should concentrate its attention upon the existing domestic depression. But while the United States was concerned with its own economic problems, an American foreign policy based upon new moral and legal assumptions with regard to the Far East was being initiated. It pointed ultimately toward an eventual involvement in the Far East, where the United States historically had only a minor economic stake.[3]

During the 1930's several determining factors also led to a sharp reversal in Japan's foreign policy. Externally, the steady development of Chinese nationalism loomed as a threat to Japan's influence on the mainland while the resumption of Sino-Russian relations late in 1932 appeared as a prophetic warning to the Tokyo government. Internally, Japan's pressing need for raw materials, in addition to finding outlets for its surplus population and industrial exports, strengthened the position of Japanese chauvinists and militarists who sought to eliminate the economic distress at home and to re-establish the country's prestige abroad.[4]

It was upon these essential factors, therefore, that the Japanese militarists provoked a clash with Chinese troops near Mukden with the intention of controlling all of Manchuria. The Chinese government immediately appealed to the League of Nations in a vain effort to marshal world opinion against the Japanese attack. A Commission of Inquiry headed by Lord Lytton was appointed to investigate the crisis and in October, 1932, its findings were made public. The Lytton Report frankly described China's failure to control Manchuria and recognized Japan's economic and strategic interests there, but the commission categorically condemned the methods used by the Japanese to correct these grievances. The report suggested that China's sovereignty be re-instituted in Manchuria and that Japanese interests and rights be protected in the process. The recommendation was totally unacceptable in Tokyo and before the report was considered at Geneva, Japan formally recognized Manchuria as the new state of Manchukuo. On February 24, 1933, the League of Nations Assembly voted that Manchuria still fell within Chinese control and censured Japan for violating the League's Covenant. At this point, Japan withdrew from the League permanently.[5]

News of the Manchurian affair caught Washington somewhat by surprise. Neither President Herbert Hoover nor his Secretary of State, Henry L. Stimson, were willing to undertake any concerted action which might lead to war; they sought some preventative method that would bring moral pressure to bear upon Japan. The idea of employing economic sanctions as an effective means of enforcing peace was ruled out by Hoover since he was convinced that such efforts would involve the nation in dangerous complications. A legalistic device was adopted instead in January, 1932, whereby the United States would not "admit the legality nor recognize any treaty which impaired its rights in China or which violated the Kellogg-Briand Pact." The Hoover-Stimson Non-recognition Doctrine was received with little enthusiasm domestically or among the European powers with interests in China. the doctrine's major opposition at home stemmed from apathy and a simplified traditional view that international involvement was not in the national interest. Great Britain, deeply concerned with economic problems of its own, was also unwilling to become embroiled in a Far Eastern crisis and remained cool to any suggestions for a joint policy with the United States.[6]

Although Stimpson's attempts at moral sanctions had little effect at home and abroad, he was successful in convincing President-elect Franklin D. Roosevelt to continue the non-recognition policy of Manchukuo. Isolationist groups now became alarmed that Roosevelt would involve the nation in a righteous crusade to halt Japanese aggression, but with the nation absorbed in domestic prostration and with Japan solidifying her position in Manchukuo, the Far Eastern tension lessened for the time being. Yet both Roosevelt and his Secretary of State, Cordell Hull, were committed in resisting further Japanese encroachments on China and as such, refused to retreat from the open door policy. Equally determined to fulfill its economic ambitions, Japan by February, 1934, established exclusive commercial enterprises in Manchukuo over repeated protests from Washington that such restrictive controls contravened American rights. The Japanese government answered these protests by declaring that those nations which had refused to recognize Manchukuo had forfeited their rights to economic equality with the new state. In short, Tokyo had rejected both the Hoover-Stimson Doctrine, and the open door policy in the Far East.[7]

Notes

[1] Ruhl J. Bartlett (ed.), *The Record of American Diplomacy: Documents and Readings in the History of American Foreign Relations* (New York: Alfred A. Knopf, 1964), pp. 489-490.

[2] *Ibid.*, pp. 490-491.

[3] William L. Newmann, *America Encounters Japan: From Perry to MacArthur* (Baltimore: The Johns Hopkins Press, 1963), p. 185.

[4] Richard W. Leopold, *The Growth of American Foreign Policy: A History* (New York: Alfred A. Knopf, 1962), pp. 521-522.

[5] *Ibid.*, pp. 522-523.

[6] Neumann, pp. 194-198; Richard N. Current, *Secretary Stimson: A Study in Statescraft* (New Brunswick: Rutgers University Press, 1954), p. 113.

[7] *Ibid.*, pp. 117-120; Robert A. Divine, *The Reluctant Belligerent: American Entry into World War II* (New York: John Wiley and Sons, Inc., 1965), p. 4; see also Leopold, p. 523.

CHAPTER I

THE APPROACHING STORM

By the beginning of 1937, Japan's economic situation had failed to improve in Asia while militant nationalism in Japan continued to gain in strength and influence. The success attained in the Manchurian conflict in 1931, the growing world economic depression, and the rise of the Nazis in Germany did encourage the expansionist elements in Japan. The easy victories already gained in China and the existing strife in Europe were a further incentive to the Japanese militarists. Nor did the prevalent American attitude based on isolationism and indifference go unnoticed. What the Japanese needed, however, was an opportunity to justify to the world any further military action to be taken in China. This opportunity was not long in coming. Taking advantage of a minor skirmish at the Marco Polo Bridge near Peking, which paralleled the Manchurian affair six years earlier, Japanese forces attacked the Chinese during the early morning of July 7, 1937.[1]

Following the outbreak of hostilities in North China the United States was faced with two essential problems: what methods should be used to protect American nationals residing in China and whether or not the provisions of the Neutrality Act should be invoked. Underlying these immediate problems was the fundamental issue as to whether the United States could continue in its isolationist attitude while at the same time pursuing its open door policy and treaty rights in China. A third alternative open to the United States was the possible cooperation with other nations in an attempt to contain Japanese aggression.[2]

Five days following the clash near Peking, Secretary of State Cordell Hull informed both the Japanese ambassador and the counselor of the Chinese Embassy that the American government would regard "an armed conflict as a great blow to the cause of peace and world progress."[3] On July 16, Hull issued a formal

6

declaration of the principles which would be advocated by the United States. Though not aimed specifically at either belligerent, it became obvious that the principles were intended as a warning to Japanese aggression. The American policy which Hull pointed out was based on the following 13 principles:

1. Maintenance of peace
2. National and international self-restraint
3. Abstinence from use of force in pursuit of policy
4. Abstinence from interference in the internal affairs of other nations
5. Adjustment of problems in international relations by processes of peaceful negotiations and agreement
6. Faithful observance of international agreements
7. Modification of provisions of treaties by orderly processes arrived at in the spirit of mutual helpfulness and accommodation
8. Respect by all nations for the rights of others and performance by all nations of established obligations
9. Revitalization and strengthening of international law
10. Promotion of economic security and stability the world over
11. Removal of excessive barriers of international trade
12. Effective equality of commercial opportunity and application of the principles of equality of treatment
13. Limitation and reduction of armament.[4]

These statements were forwarded to other governments of the world for consideration and comment in an effort to marshal world opinion against the threat of war in the Far East. Comments were received from more than 60 nations and, except for Portugal, which emphatically condemned any attempt to solve critical problems by such a vague and ambiguous formula, most of the governments expressed their approval of the secretary's principles. Japan replied that it also concurred in the program as formulated by Hull. The Japanese government, however, made one important reservation when it informed the American State Department that the objectives of these principles "would only be attained in their application to the Far Eastern situation by a full recognition and practical consideration of the actual particular circumstances of that region. . . ."[5]

In other words, the Japanese government made it painfully clear to Hull that it would concur with the principles as they applied to the world in general but would not abide by them if the program interfered with Japan's aspirations in China. Indeed, the recent action taken by the Japanese military had the full support not only of the cabinet but also of the leaders in the Diet, political parties, press, and business interests as well. Writing about the crisis years later, Joseph Grew, the American Ambassador to Japan, reiterated this feeling when he declared that "at no time during my service in Japan had I observed indications of so strong and unanimous a determination on the part of the Japanese government to maintain Japan's position in North China even if extensive hostilities became necessary."[6] Grew hoped that any action taken by the United States in the conflict would be made only if it did not aggravate the already tense situation there or place American citizens and property in jeopardy as a result of the war. Even after a month of fighting, Grew felt that the situation had not sufficiently developed to warrant a recommendation for any action other than attempting to find a peaceful solution to the dilemma in China.[7]

A peaceful solution was sought as early as July 20 when Sir Ronald Lindsay, the British Ambassador to the United States, proposed that the Western nations approach the Japanese and Chinese governments with a request that they suspend all further troop movements and agree to an immediate armistice. The United States, on July 21, approved the British proposal and, on the same day, Hull informed the warring governments that the United States would welcome any suggestions for assistance which could be rendered in order to seek a solution to the controversy. Even Japan's projected allies, Germany and Italy, attempted to end hostilities in the Orient. Though a policy of strict neutrality was maintained, the German Foreign Office strongly desired an early settlement of the difficulties for the sake of "German economic aspirations in the Far East and in view of the anti-Comintern policy." The German government believed that the continuation of the conflict would benefit only the Soviets, who welcomed Japanese entanglement in China since it would alleviate any potential concentration of Japanese forces on Russia's eastern borders. The official Italian attitude regarding the Far Eastern conflict was strikingly similar to the German point of view. Attempts by the Fascist governments at mediation systematically diminished as the war progressed and Japanese victories mounted in China. In November, the Japanese government did suggest a peace proposal which would be conducted under the auspices of the German Foreign Office, but the fall of Nanking to their forces in December terminated any hope for a negotiated peace.[8]

Meanwhile, Hull instructed Grew in early August to inform

\Kiko\ Hirota, the Japanese Foreign Minister, that the good offices of the American government would be offered in settling the dispute between China and Japan. Hirota was cool toward the offer and replied that the most effective action that could be taken by the United States would be to persuade the Chinese government to make peace proposals immediately to Japan. These proposals, however, never came about and plans for mediating a peace were now abandoned by the United States.[9]

Anthony Eden, the British Foreign Minister, informed his ambassador in Nanking that since neither side sought the good offices of Great Britain, the English government would also abstain from offering mediation. But in Shanghai the British did attempt to arrange a truce, although this was in no way an effort to intervene in the crisis. Economically, they had millions of pounds presently invested in Shanghai, and any concentrated fighting there would jeopardize that investment. The British also hoped to keep the fighting from the city, which was congested with non-combatants. The British legation, therefore, proposed that all belligerent troops be withdrawn from the area while the foreign powers presently residing in the city assume responsibility for the safety of Japanese and other civilians in Shanghai. The Chinese agreed to this proposal, but the Japanese declined on the grounds that their government would be responsible for its nationals. Moreover, since the Japanese believed that the crisis in the area was entirely due to continuous Chinese attacks, they felt that the inadequate foreign armed forces in Shanghai were not sufficiently strong enough to sustain a concentrated attack.[10]

On August 20, the Japanese Premier, Prince Konoye, defined Japanese policy in China by declaring that the situation must be settled without foreign intervention "for the sake of Japan's future relations with China." In Shanghai, in particular, he claimed that Japan merely sought to eliminate the anti-Japanese feeling which existed there. Hirota reiterated these policies when he announced in the Diet on September 3 that "Japan's objective is to obtain from China a drastic improvement of her attitude towards this country. . . . We are fighting the anti-Japanese movement in China. We want to see China governed by statesmen who can maintain friendly relations with us."[11]

Prior to Hirota's announcement, Admiral Harry E. Yarnell, Commander of the United States Asiatic Fleet, requested that 1,200 Marines be dispatched to Shanghai to protect American citizens and property—a request which President Roosevelt and his secretary of state approved. Simultaneously, isolationists in Congress demanded a complete withdrawal of American armed forces from China as a further step to enforce American neutrality policies in the Far East. At a press conference on August 17, Hull warned that if American forces were withdrawn from Shanghai, American civilians residing there would be exposed to the armies of both belligerents and left defenseless. Moreover, the secretary believed that such a move would merely create the impression of weakness on the part of the United States in the eyes of world opinion. "We frankly do not feel disposed," Hull declared, "by leaning back too far the other way, to give other countries a chance to suppose or to suggest that we are cowardly."[12] Hull further pointed out that American military detachments in China were assigned there by treaty rights, specifically under the provisions of the Boxer Protocol of 1901. When hostilities broke out in July, the United States had 528 marines stationed in Peking, 786 soldiers in Tientsin and 1,073 marines in Shanghai—the latter to protect American nationals residing in the International Settlement.[13]

American naval detachments, on the other hand, had been stationed in China as early as 1866 under the provisions of the Sino-American Treaty of 1858 which provided protection for what little commercial and missionary interests existed at that time. These interests were expanded following the Spanish-American War and additional gunboats were added to the newly-created Yangtze Patrol which became a subdivision of the United States Asiatic Fleet in 1901. First mention of the Yangtze Patrol appeared in the annual report of the secretary of the navy in 1920 when he stated that the purpose of the patrol was to "defend vessels from river pirates and lawless elements who were holding up and looting steamers and junks and firing on passing craft." During the period 1927-1928, following a wave of nationalist reaction in central China, the Yangtze Patrol was involved in no less than 37 skirmishes in its efforts to protect foreign lives and property. The Navy Department, as a counter to this threat, strengthened the patrol, which in early 1928 consisted of one light cruiser, two minesweepers, three gunboats and ten light destroyers. The Nationalists, led by Chiang Kai-Shek, consolidated their position in the Yangtze Valley by 1928 and soon became the de facto government of half of China. Order was eventually restored to the war-torn area by the Nationalist Chinese but as a safeguard against further upheavals, the Navy Department by the end of 1928 approved the construction in Shanghai of six new American

gunboats, including the *USS Panay*. Following the outbreak of
hostilities in July, 1937, the Yangtze Patrol's essential mission and
purpose was restated by the secretary of state on August 10:

> United States armed forces have no mission of offensive action
> against the armed forces of any other country, nor is it one of
> coercion of foreign governments. Their primary function is protect-
> ing American nationals, secondarily, American property. They are
> not expected to hold their position at any hazard, nor against a
> responsibly directed armed force of any country operating on express
> higher authority.[14]

With the outbreak of war in China, isolationists sought to
invoke the Third Neutrality Act.* On July 29, Senator Key
Pittman, chairman of the Senate Foreign Relations Committee,
issued a formal statement declaring that every armed conflict which
broke out in the world was not a formal declaration of war. But
he pointed out that the protection given to Americans in China
would be reduced if the neutrality legislation were applied. Moreover, protection of American nationals there would be made
difficult if a state of war were recognized by the United States.
Twenty-four members of the House, however, issued a joint declaration urging Congress to remain in session and to take "every
possible action to protect this country against becoming involved
in the Far Eastern war." At the same time, peace societies and
other pacifist groups opposed to American involvement in the
Orient also exerted pressure on Congress and the Administration.[15]

Replying to this criticism, Secretary Hull indicated that the
American government would facilitate a safe removal of its
nationals from the war zone in China and in the process would
afford its citizens all the military protection that was felt necessary.
Reiterating his July 16 statement of policy, he placated isolationists
somewhat by announcing that the government was making every
effort to pursue "the policies of peace in which this country
believes and to which it is committed. . . ."[16]

Hull meanwhile requested that American naval detachments
in the Shanghai area continue to protect American nationals while
avoiding the war zone as much as possible. On August 25, Admiral
Hasegawa, the Japanese naval commander, issued a formal state-

---

* By the terms of the Third Neutrality Act, which was passed by Congress
in May, 1937, if the President found a state of war to exist, he was compelled
to place an embargo on war materials, a ban on American loans, and to prohibit
travel by American citizens on belligerent vessels. The act also gave the President discretionary authority to place all trade with belligerents on a cash and
carry basis. Robert A. Divine, *The Reluctant Belligerent: American Entry into
World War II* (New York: John Wiley and Sons, Inc., 1965), p. 4.

ment to the effect that navigation along the lower Yangtze River
and along the central Chinese coast would be closed to Chinese
shipping even though foreign vessels would still be allowed in the
area. Since Chinese vessels had been flying foreign flags in an
effort to avoid capture, it was further announced by the Japanese
on August 26 that advance notice was to be given of all vessels
entering the war zone, in addition to the name of the particular
ship and the purpose for which it was entering the blockaded area.
Eden in a note to Hull suggested that the United States, Great
Britain, and France agree to the halting of their respective
merchant vessels by Japanese ships to verify their nationality, but
only with the understanding that:

1. Verification would be undertaken by Japanese war ships only
   if a war vessel of the neutral is not readily available.
2. Verification would not occur frequently and that the Japanese
   would not misuse the privilege.

Joint action was not suggested by Eden if a conflict over such
verification occurred, but separate representations instead would
be made to the Japanese government.[17]

In answer to Eden's request, the secretary of state at the outset
maintained that "the Japanese have no right to overhaul vessels of
third powers." Hull felt, however, that few cases would actually
occur where foreign vessels would be halted for verification, since
mere observation would identify the nationality of the ship. Hull
believed that none of the foreign powers would resist verification
by retaliatory measures even though the halting of their vessels
would accord to the Japanese a privilege inconsistent with the
rules of international law. The secretary of state in general
accepted Eden's proposals, but there were two influencing factors
to consider: that however limited Japan's enforcement of a
blockade might be at the beginning, it might soon become more
extensive and produce a crisis and, secondly, if the British proposal
were accepted *in toto* it would violate American neutrality laws.
For these reasons, Hull decided to adopt parallel action instead,
a move which Eden accepted. The French government, on the
other hand, believed the adoption of the verification policy "would
be equivalent to acknowledging that a state of war exists in the
Far East and as such would have repercussions in the Mediterranean
area." The French instead proposed that merchant vessels entering
the blockaded area notify the Japanese authorities of such entry
giving the name of the vessel and its captain and the cargo being
transported. They further suggested that such a plan be adopted

simultaneously by the Western democracies. The French proposal, however, was rejected by both Great Britain and the United States.[18]

On August 28, Admiral Yarnell requested from Admiral William D. Leahy, the Chief of Naval Operations, that heavy cruisers be dispatched to the Asiatic Fleet as an additional safeguard to American interests in China. Leahy conferred with Roosevelt and Hull over the request but both vetoed such a move. Roosevelt believed that "there is some danger of losing important units of the fleet if they should be sent to China at this time." The President instead favored sending a merchant vessel in order to hasten the evacuation of American nationals from the war zone. Hull further elaborated on Roosevelt's policy by declaring that a naval reinforcement would surely provoke the belligerents involved and ultimately cause complications from either an accidental or intentional attack upon one of the vessels. Such an incident, Hull believed, would bring about a storm of protests from isolationists in the United States. Leahy, on the other hand, favored the strengthening of American forces in the Far East and firmly believed that it ". . . appears inevitable that a major war between the Occident and the Orient must be faced at some time now or in the future."[19]

By September 5, the Japanese government issued further proclamations which extended the blockade over the entire coastal area of China and requested that advance notice be given by neutral vessels entering or leaving the mainland. The British government, although refusing to recognize such action taken by the Japanese, informed the American charge d' affaires in London on September 6 that it would acquiesce to the proposals on the following conditions:

1. If a British warship is present when British merchant vessels are halted by the Japanese in order to verify the right of that vessel to fly the British flag.
2. If no British warship is present, the Japanese will then be justified in questioning the validity of merchant vessels through search. The British government, however, reserves the right to claim compensation for any damages sustained in the process.
3. The British government will advise their merchant vessels to be searched by the Japanese if no British warship is in the vicinity provided that an immediate report is made to British naval authorities.[20]

The American charge d' affairs in Great Britain informed Hull that the British government intended to avoid any potential conflict which might evolve in the Far East. "Conditions in Europe and the Mediterranean," the American minister wrote, "are so full of potential danger that any policy other than one of caution and conciliation in the Sino-Japanese situation is virtually impossible."[21]

Finding itself in a precarious position, the American State Department followed the British pronouncement by issuing formal instructions regarding verification of commercial vessels in the blockaded area:

1. That the commander of the Asiatic Fleet inform the Japanese authorities of the expected movements of American vessels in and around the blockaded zone
2. That if American vessels are halted by Japanese authorities, the masters should produce evidence of nationality but should submit to further investigation only after a protest is lodged to the commander of the Asiatic Fleet or to the nearest American authorities.[22]

Like the British, the United States attempted to correct any potential dangers which might occur over verification of neutral shipping. Indeed, Roosevelt went one step further than the British by issuing a proclamation on September 14 prohibiting merchant vessels from transporting any implements of war to both belligerents and stating that to do so would be at their own risk. In this respect, the President attempted to abide by the Neutrality Act of May, 1937, and so quiet fears of isolationists as well as thwart another possible area of conflict, particularly with Japan.[23]

Chinese vessels meanwhile continued to defy the Japanese blockade of the China coast by having their ships' registration transferred to neutral countries. The Japanese Foreign Office informed the neutral nations that the validity of such transfers would not be recognized, citing the proclamation of August 25 which legalized such transfers only if they were made in accordance with the laws of the countries concerned. The United States, however, was not involved, since no Chinese vessel secured an American registration on or before the deadline. Vitally concerned with the announcement, the British denied the validity of the Japanese proposal by declaring that if a valid transfer occurred, the fact that it took place after August 25 was irrelevant. For this reason, the British government refused to accept the Japanese pronouncement and any subsequent solution to this dilemma was not found by either country.[24]

By the middle of September, Japanese forces advanced within striking distance of Nanking. Foreigners were still residing in the

city and non-belligerent vessels were plying the waters nearby. As
early as August 23, the Japanese government informed both the
American and British embassies that foreign warships and merchant vessels in the Nanking area should be plainly marked in
order that identification from the air could be made easier. To
this request, both governments complied in an effort to avoid any
incidents of mistaken identity.[25] As Japanese troops drew closer
to Nanking, foreigners were strongly warned to withdraw in order
to avoid projected aerial attacks upon the city, while neutral
nations were requested to remove their vessels from the area.
Commenting on Japan's announcement and warning to all foreigners to leave Nanking because of aerial bombing, Leahy asserted:

> Compliance of the American government with the demands of
> Japan in her undeclared war of aggression against China will almost
> certainly lose for America much of the high regard in which they
> have heretofore been held by the Chinese.

In view of this renewed crisis, the British government again
called for collective action. In a memorandum of September 15,
the State Department, though in complete accord with the British
desire "to keep alive in the Far Eastern area the principle of international law with regard to maritime law," believed that if such
measures were taken the Japanese government would formally
declare war on China and thereby claim belligerent rights. The
State Department further indicated that since merchant vessels
had not been attacked from the air by Japanese forces since the
outbreak of hostilities, any collective action at the present time
would not be opportune nor would it serve any useful purpose.
In this respect, what the State Department hoped to adopt was a
wait-and-see policy regarding the crisis between Japan and China.
Leahy criticized such a plan and indicated that the opportunity
to check Japan would be lost if the United States failed to take
positive action in the Far East.[26]

By the end of September, extensive Japanese air raids on
Nanking had endangered not only foreign embassies but foreign
nationals and property as well. Warnings were issued by the
Japanese military commander urging foreign officials and residents
to withdraw from the city and into areas of greater safety before
noon on September 19. On the following day, Admiral Yarnell
informed Admiral Hasegawa that American vessels would remain
in Nanking as long as American nationals remained in the city
and therefore warned him to advise his aviators accordingly. In a
show of determination, Yarnell dispatched the *USS Panay* to

Nanking on September 21 to protect and assist American nationals in the area. On September 22, the Japanese launched an extensive air raid upon the city which immediately brought a strong protest from Hull. "This government," the secretary of state declared, "holds the view that any general bombing of an extensive area wherein there resides a large populace engaged in peaceful pursuits is unwarranted and contrary to principles of law and of humanity." Hull informed the Japanese that since Nanking was the seat of the Chinese government, any withdrawal from the area would greatly hinder American diplomatic functions there. Nor would a withdrawal up-river, for that matter, insure the safety of American officials and non-combatants from further extensive raids by the Japanese. "The American government," the secretary stated, ". . . expresses the earnest hope that future bombings in and around the city of Nanking will be avoided."[27]

Strong protests were also lodged by Great Britain, France, Germany, and Italy, while the Soviet Union made it clear that it would hold the Japanese accountable for any damage to its embassy in Nanking. In reply to these protests, Hirota indicated that Japanese forces would specifically avoid any attacks upon non-belligerents, although how this was to be done in view of the massive bombing raids that were occurring was not disclosed. His formal reply to Hull on September 29, however, bluntly rejected the American proposal to halt the aerial attacks upon Nanking:

> The bombing of Nanking is a necessary and unavoidable measure for the attainment of the military objectives of the Japanese forces. The rights and interests of third countries . . . would be respected as far as possible, but injury might be unavoidable notwithstanding the greatest precautions which might be taken by Japanese forces.

Hull realized that if the State Department issued stronger protests in connection with the Nanking bombing at this point it would not only lead to a diplomatic break but would also risk the disapproval of a predominantly isolationist Congress and of the public at large. Indeed, in a Gallup Poll taken in September regarding public sympathy in the Sino-Japanese conflict, 55 percent ostensibly remained indifferent to the crisis, while in another poll the following month 69 percent favored stricter neutrality laws. But Hull refused to acquiesce to indiscriminate attacks upon non-combatants in the Nanking area and therefore remained poised and ready to object to any further bombings of the Chinese capital.[28]

At this juncture, the League of Nations displayed a growing concern over the Sino-Japanese conflict and appointed an advisory committee to deal with the crisis. On September 27, the committee protested the Japanese bombing of what it called open cities and expressed "profound distress at the loss of life caused to innocent civilians including great numbers of women and children." By early October, upon the recommendation of the advisory committee, the League of Nations Assembly adopted and published its findings which in essence declared Japan guilty of violating the terms of the Nine Power Treaty of 1922 and the Pact of Paris of 1928. The State Department immediately issued a statement that the United States agreed with the League's conclusions.[29]

The Japanese government countered the conclusions reached in the League Assembly by declaring that the crisis was precipitated from an attack by Chinese forces upon a Japanese garrison stationed legitimately in North China by treaty. Indeed, the Japanese government firmly believed it had done everything possible to reach an amicable settlement over the Marco Polo Bridge incident. The statement further affirmed their intention of ending what it termed the anti-Japanese attitude existing in China and establishing closer cooperation between the two Oriental nations. For these reasons, Japan sincerely believed it had violated neither the Nine Power Treaty nor the Pact of Paris.[30]

What action the League would now take depended largely upon the attitude of the Western powers, particularly the United States. In conjunction with the League's conclusions and as a direct result of the aerial bombing of Nanking, Roosevelt, on October 5, delivered his "quarantine" speech in Chicago. The President called upon the peace-loving nations to make a concerted effort "to protect the sanctity of international treaties and to maintain international morality." Precisely what Roosevelt had in mind in his quarantine theory remained undefined, though he may have been thinking of some sort of collective security against aggression. The President seemed convinced, however, that the United States could no longer remain complacent to growing global tensions, and that the government could not continue its isolationist policy while American interests and property were being threatened in China.

The immediate reaction to his speech was divided both at home and abroad. Advocates of international measures to restrain aggressors were heartened by the speech and hoped that the government would undertake a program which would serve as a deterrent to Japanese expansionist plans. The American Committee for Non-Participation in Japanese Aggression believed that an economic embargo would not only weaken Japan's capacity to wage war in China but that it would curb Japanese expansion. "It is inconsistent with our own interest," the committee declared, "to supply Japan the sinews of war and then to spend huge sums on naval armaments in order to counteract the growth in aggressive power which we are helping to make possible." In their annual conference held in Atlantic City, the National Maritime Union of America passed a resolution calling upon the Federal government to "enforce an economic embargo on Japan . . . and to forbid the importation into this country of all goods manufactured in countries controlled by the Japanese government. . . ."[31]

Admiral Leahy further urged the free nations to launch consolidated measures against Japan before "they (the Japanese) become too firmly entrenched in China."[32] This call for collective action was discussed in official British circles and Prime Minister Neville Chamberlain, on October 8, announced that the British would cooperate with the United States in containing aggression in the Orient. Eden reinforced this policy when he announced in the House of Commons that any British action in the Far East would parallel American efforts. The foreign minister, however, was well aware that the strong isolationist influence prevailing in the United States would disapprove of any positive measure that might be undertaken.[33] The German ambassador also felt that the United States would not intervene actively in the Far East because of the widespread isolationist sentiment in the country. Ambassador Hans Dieckhoff believed the American government would abandon its present policy only if a world conflict occurred which involved Great Britain.[34]

Japanese Ambassador Saito, in a meeting with Hull, insisted that the Japanese had not violated the Nine Power Treaty, since China had consistently broken agreements which forced Japan to adopt armed intervention. Saito, with Roosevelt's speech in mind, asserted that the Japanese government sought a conciliatory end to the fighting but that consistent interference by non-belligerents had made matters worse.[35]

The quarantine speech, however, received widespread disapproval from a pacifist-inclined Congress and an isolationist public. Indeed, the very term "quarantine" produced a sense of alarm among many Americans who hoped to avoid anything that resembled involvement in the Far-Eastern crisis. It was a general belief that, by defending American property and legal rights in China, the United States would become embroiled in the political

issues of the conflict and would lead ultimately to active participation in the war. Particularly related to maintaining the status
quo there was the presence of American river gunboats directly
in the path of hostilities. Isolationists viewed their presence with
grave misgivings since any involvement with Japanese forces might
produce an incident embarrassing to both nations. This fear was
pointed out in an editorial by *Current History* magazine which
declared prophetically that "should a national be killed or a unit
of the Asiatic squadron be sunk it is highly probable that American
public opinion, fanned by sensational publicity, would be aroused
to a dangerous pitch where an accident might lead to war."[36]

Senator William Borah of Idaho, in leading the opposition in
Congress, declared that levying sanctions against Japan would be
"just the same as initiating war," while the editorial opinion of
the Hearst newspapers believed Roosevelt was being manipulated
to salvage the British Empire in the Far East. Grew, who consistently favored a policy of non-involvement, was disappointed by
the President's speech. Moral judgments, he was certain, would
not restrain aggression and he believed that America would surely
be involved in the Far Eastern war if a policy of collective security
were attempted.[37]

Roosevelt was astonished by the widespread criticism to his
quarantine speech and indignant that even many members of his
own party refused to support this policy. "It is a terrible thing,"
he told one of his close advisors, "to look over your shoulder
when you are trying to lead and find no one there."[38] Domestic
reaction forced the President to shelve any thoughts of collective
security at this time but he remained thoroughly convinced that
the United States, to protect its interests, could no longer maintain an aloof and indifferent attitude in the Far East. In a conversation with a visiting French statesman, Roosevelt remained skeptical that the continuation of a neutrality policy under any circumstances would give the United States permanent security. Such
a plan, he asserted, was full of pitfalls that could well lead to
involvement.

Roosevelt expressed a similar attitude in a letter to Edward
M. House on October 19. "I verily believe," he told House, "that
as time goes on we can slowly but surely make people realize
that war will be a greater danger to us if we close all the doors
and windows than if we go out in the street and use our influence
to curb the riot."[39]

The League of Nations Far Eastern Advisory Committee continued to seek a solution to the Sino-Japanese dispute and as such called upon the signers of the Nine Power Treaty to meet in a conference at Brussels on November 4. Invitations were also extended to nine other nations, including Germany and the Soviet Union. Though Germany refrained from showing any partiality for Japan, she displayed a neutral outlook by declining the invitation. The German government believed that a policy of neutrality rather than interventionism should govern the Western attitude in the Far East. Therefore, it left Italy to support Japan at the conference. The Soviet Union attended, but its envoy, Litvinov, departed before the conference ended, since he felt the meeting would not accomplish any material results.[40]

Norman Davis was appointed by Roosevelt as the American representative to the conference and assurances were made to an anxious nation that the United States "will enter the conference without any commitments on the part of this government to other governments." Although the President and his secretary of state were determined to keep the nation out of war in the Far East, they hoped, nevertheless, that the conference would exert moral pressure upon Japan to alter her attitude and policy in China. Commenting on the anticipated meeting, Leahy believed that if pressure were brought to bear upon Japan by the conference members, the United States would not be forced to undertake the problem without assistance. The chief of naval operations felt, however, that any condemnations issued would have no effect upon Japan and that any direct action such as embargoes or sanctions would virtually be a declaration of war.[41]

Repeated attempts subsequently were made by the conference to persuade Japan to send a delegate to the meeting, but as Sir Robert Craigie, the British Ambassador to Tokyo observed, the Japanese adopted a belligerent attitude from the start. In an official statement to the conference, the Japanese government contended that "the conflict between Japan and China is outside the scope of the Nine Power Treaty. . . ." The Japanese, therefore, made it emphatically clear that the conflict could be settled only by direct negotiations between the two countries involved and that any interference from the Western nations would not be permitted. The conspicuous absence of Japan ultimately dealt a deathblow to any practical policies that might have been adopted by the conference. Moreover, the United States refused to initiate economic sanctions on its own if this meant protecting the possessions of other nations in Asia from possible reprisals by the

Japanese. Such a policy would be more distasteful to isolationists than imposing sanctions. Even the Scandanavian countries refrained from approving any specific economic policies against Japan; the Italian delegate believed such an undertaking would merely lead to serious complications. The conference, which concluded on November 24, failed to accomplish its immediate objective. At best, it reaffirmed the principles of the Nine Power Treaty and urged both belligerents to settle their differences in accordance with those principles, advice which Japan conveniently ignored. Roosevelt, nonetheless, felt that the conference did succeed in emphasizing the indifference which the Japanese government displayed concerning the terms of the Washington Conference of 1922.[42]

Notes

[1] Richard W. Van Alstyne, *American Diplomacy in Action* (Stanford: Stanford University Press, 1944), pp. 341-342.

[2] Thomas A. Bisson, *American Policy in the Far East, 1931-1940* (New York: Institute of Pacific Relations, Inquiry Series, 1940), p. 57.

[3] *Ibid.*

[4] U.S., Department of State, *Peace and War, United States Foreign Policy, 1931-1941* (Washington: GPO, 1943), II, 46. Cited hereafter as *Peace and War, 1931-1941.*

[5] *Ibid.*

[6] Joseph C. Grew, *Turbulent Era* (Boston: Houghton Mifflin Company, 1952), II, 1039.

[7] *Ibid.*, p. 1043.

[8] Charles C. Tansill, *Back Door to War: The Roosevelt Foreign Policy, 1933-1941* (Chicago: Henry Regnery Company, 1952), pp. 481-484.

[9] *Peace and War, 1931-1941*, p. 374.

[10] Frank Oliver, *Special Undeclared War* (London: Jonathan Cape, Ltd., 1939), pp. 140-141.

[11] Quoted in *Ibid.*, pp. 141-143.

[12] Cordell Hull, *The Memoirs of Cordell Hull* (New York: The Macmillan Company, 1948), I, 540-541.

[13] U.S., Department of State, *Foreign Relations of the United States, Diplomatic Papers, 1937* (Washington: GPO, 1954), III, 421. Cited hereafter as *Foreign Relations, 1937.*

[14] Kemp Tolley, "Yang-Pat-Shanghai to Chunking," *United States Naval Institute Proceedings*, 89 (June, 1963), pp. 85-87. The other five gunboats constructed were the *USS Luzon, USS Tuituila, USS Oahu, USS Guam,* and *USS Mindanao.* Prior to the outbreak of war in July, 1937, the Yangtze Patrol had been systematically reduced to ten gunboats.

[15] Bisson, p. 60.

[16] *Peace and War, 1931-1941*, pp. 375-376.

[17] *Foreign Relations, 1937*, pp. 434-440.

[18] *Ibid.*, p. 442, 447.

[19] William D. Leahy, Diary, August 24-28, 1937, William D. Leahy Papers, Manuscript Division, Library of Congress. Cited hereafter as Leahy Papers.

[20] *Foreign Relations, 1937*, p. 455.

[21] *Ibid.*

[22] W. A. Angwin, "The China Incident," pp. 84-85, Unpublished manuscript in the Harry E. Yarnell Papers, Manuscript Division, Library of Congress. Cited hereafter as Yarnell Papers.

[23] U.S., President, 1933-1945 (Roosevelt), *Development of United States Foreign Policy: Addresses and Messages of Franklin D. Roosevelt*, Senate Publication No. 188 (Washington: GPO, 1943), p. 354.

[24] *Foreign Relations, 1937*, pp. 465-467.

[25] *Ibid.*, p. 458.

[26] Leahy Diary, September 21, 1937, Leahy Papers. See also *Foreign Relations, 1937*, p. 463.

[27] Bisson, p. 63.

[28] *Ibid.*, pp. 63-64. See also George Gallup and Claude Robinson, "Public Opinion Surveys, 1935-1938," *The Public Opinion Quarterly,* 2 (July, 1938), 223.

[29] Hull, I, 543-544.

[30] S. Shepard Jones and Denys P. Meyers, *Documents on American Foreign Relations,* (Boston: World Peace Foundation, 1939), I, 163-164.

[31] *America's Share in Japan's War Guilt* (New York: American Committee for Non-Participation in Japanese Aggression, 1938), pp. 16, 53.

[32] Leahy Diary, October 6, 1937, Leahy Papers.

[33] Irving S. Friedman, *British Relations With China, 1931-1939* (New York: Institute of Pacific Relations, 1940), pp. 102-103.

[34] Jones and Meyers, I, 641.

[35] Conversation between Cordell Hull and Hiroshi Saito, October 7, 1937, Cordell Hull Papers, Manuscript Division, Library of Congress, Box 229. Cited hereafter as Hull Papers.

[36] *Current History and Forum,* 47 (October, 1937), p. 13.

[37] S. Jules Davids, *America and the World of Our Time: Diplomacy in the Twentieth Century* (New York: Random House, 1960), p. 165.

[38] Alexander De Conde, *A History of American Foreign Policy* (New York: Charles Scribner's Sons, 1963), p. 571.

[39] William L. Langer and S. Everett Gleason, *The Challenge to Isolation, 1937-1940* (New York: Harper and Brothers, 1952), p. 24. See also Elliott Roosevelt (ed.), *F.D.R. His Personal Letters, 1928-1945* (New York: Duell, Sloan and Pearce, 1950), I, 719.

[40] Arnold J. Toynbee, *Survey of International Affairs* (London: Oxford University Press, 1938), I, 299; see also Harriet L. Moore, *Soviet Far Eastern Policy, 1931-1945* (Princeton: Princeton University Press, 1945), p. 89.

[41] Samuel I. Rosenman (ed.), *The Public Papers and Addresses of Franklin D. Roosevelt* (New York: The Macmillan Company, 1941), VI, 436. See also Leahy Diary, October 16, 1937, Leahy Papers.

[42] *Peace and War, 1931-1941,* p. 390; see also Grew, p. 189; David, p. 165; Robert L. Craigie, *Behind the Japanese Mask* (London: Hutchinson Ltd., 1945), pp. 9, 51; Raymond L. Buell, *Isolated America* (New York: Alfred A. Knopf, Inc., 1940), p. 110; Rosenman, pp. 463-464.

CHAPTER II

THE CRISIS

While the Brussels Conference was attempting to bring about an end to the conflict in China, Japanese forces methodically continued to advance toward Nanking. Warnings were issued to all foreigners by the Japanese government to withdraw from the city pending a large-scale ground attack that would soon occur. On November 22, 1937, the various foreign ambassadors and ministers, along with many of their nationals, departed further inland to Hankow while the American ambassador and part of his staff left for that city on board the *USS Luzon,* flagship of the Yangtze Patrol. The rest of the American Embassy staff stayed in Nanking in order to keep the embassy operating as long as possible and to render any assistance to Americans who remained in the besieged city. On the same day, the *USS Panay* received instructions to remain at Nanking so that communications could be maintained between the embassy and the State Department and to withdraw the remaining Americans and other nationals from the city when it became vitally necessary. The American ambassador informed the Japanese government of this move and requested that "the Japanese military and civil authorities take note of these circumstances . . . and should necessity arise accord full recognition to the diplomatic status of the embassy personnel and premises there and give them appropriate facilities and full protection."[1]

On December 1, Grew appealed to Hirota to initiate steps to end the indiscriminate bombings of Nanking and the surrounding area and warned the Japanese minister of the serious effect such bombings would have upon the American people if an incident occurred involving the United States directly. Hirota informed Grew that American nationals, along with other foreigners, had been warned to leave the area of hostilities, although he would

24

inform the military authorities of Grew's appeals. In light of the steady advance of the Japanese forces toward Nanking, the Code Section of the American Embassy in the city was removed to the *Panay* on the following day.[2]

By December 7, the Japanese reached the outskirts of Tangshan, some 20 miles east of Nanking. The embassies still functioning in Nanking simultaneously agreed to withdraw aboard prepared vessels the following day. George Atcheson, Jr., who had been left behind in charge of the American Embassy, established a temporary office on board the *Panay*. Atcheson immediately informed the Japanese authorities on December 9 that 18 Americans were planning to remain in the city in connection with hospital and newspaper work. He requested therefore that "appropriate protection and facilities be given to these Americans." The American consul-general in China, C. E. Gauss, also informed the Japanese consul in Shanghai on December 10 that the *Panay* was anchored some two miles up the Yangtze River from Pukow outside Nanking and requested him to "notify your military and naval authorities the position of the vessel so that it may not be endangered by the activities of the Japanese forces."[3] While this request was being forwarded, Japanese planes had already commenced aerial bombings of the Pukow area, a procedure which compelled Lieutenant Commander J. J. Hughes, commanding the *Panay,* to move the vessel two miles further up river to San Chia Ho, near the Asiatic Petroleum Company installation, where he could meet any Americans who decided to evacuate the city. Early on December 11, the Japanese onslaught extended near the area where the *Panay* was anchored and forced the vessel to a point 12 miles above Nanking near where several British ships were anchored. Atcheson again urgently requested Gauss to inform the Japanese consul general to instruct the Japanese Air Force of the *Panay's* new position at San Chia Ho.

Later that evening Atcheson cabled Hull that Japanese artillery batteries deliberately opened fire upon the British vessels, *HMS Scarab, HMS Cricket,* the passenger steamer *Wangpoo* and the merchant launch *Woo Kuang.* The shelling continued to harass the British vessels while they attempted to sail upstream and out of range. Three Standard-Vacuum Oil Company vessels, the *SS Meiping, SS Meihsia,* and the *SS Meian,* along with the *Panay,* were also threatened by the artillery barrage, but the vessels moved safely upstream.[4]

Early in the morning of December 12 the British gunboat *HMS Ladybird* prominently displaying the Union Jack was shelled by Japanese shore batteries between Wuhu and Nanking, killing one sailor and wounding several others including the vessel's captain. The tug *Tsingtah*, which British officials had used during their evacuation of Nanking, was also machine-gunned at Wuhu by the Japanese. Later that morning, Japanese airplanes attacked the *Scarab* and *Cricket* as they lay in anchor 15 miles above Nanking but inflicted no damage. The British vigorously protested the attack upon nonbelligerent vessels, but Colonel Kingoro Hashimoto, the Japanese artillery commander, informed the British that Japanese armed forces had orders to attack all vessels in the Yangtze River. Robert Craigie, the British Ambassador to Japan, also lodged protests, and the Japanese government promised to investigate.[5]

At 9 a.m. on December 12, Japanese shell fire again compelled the *Panay* and the three Standard Oil vessels to move further upstream. Atcheson immediately informed the Japanese authorities both in Shanghai and Tokyo that the *Panay* and its convoy were forced to proceed to Hoshien some 27 miles southeast of Nanking. The Japanese consul general acknowledged receipt of this notification almost immediately. The American ambassador in Hankow also was notified of the *Panay's* movements and cabled Hull to dispatch the new position to the Japanese embassy.[6] By 10 a.m., the *Panay* had proceeded some 20 miles to the designated area but was halted by a Nipponese military unit on the north shore of the river and boarded. The boarding party sought information concerning the movements of the *Panay*, and any activities of Chinese troops sighted along the way. Hughes informed the Japanese that the convey was sailing to Hoshien and out of the path of their offensive upon Nanking but firmly impressed upon them that the United States was a non-belligerent and could not disclose the movements of Chinese forces in the area. Apparently satisfied, the Japanese boarding party departed and the *Panay* continued its fateful voyage to the designated rendezvous point. The gunboat arrived at its destination by 11 a.m., followed by the three tankers which proceeded to anchor nearby.[7] Each vessel in the convoy was identified by two horizontal 18′ x 14′ flags painted on the awnings and superstructure and visible from the air at any angle. In addition, three sizable American flags were flying. Since the day was sunny and cloudless and since the Hoshien area was ostensibly out of the mainstream of hostilities,

Hughes ordered the vessel's three-inch guns and its .30 caliber machine guns to remain covered. The crew of the *Panay* normally consisted of five officers and 50 men but the escape up the Yangtze River had expanded this number to 70. The overload were members of the embassy staff, American and foreign civilians, as well as several cameramen and newspaper correspondents.[8]

Almost immediately upon arriving at the destination, Atcheson requested Gauss to inform the Japanese Embassy at Shanghai of the convoy's exact position "in order that they may issue appropriate instructions to their forces." Atcheson further added that circumstances might compel the *Panay* to move from its position and that the gunboat expected to return to Nanking as soon as possible so that the embassy might resume its functions in the city. Gauss received this communication at 12:15 p.m.; before one o'clock, he had telephoned the Japanese consul general to whom he also sent a dispatch verifying the conversation.[9]

Meanwhile, the Twelfth and Thirteenth Japanese Naval Air Groups composed of 24 fighters and 42 single and twin engine bombers, were informed early on December 12 that an advanced Japanese ground unit had sighted several vessels fleeing the Nanking area ostensibly containing Chinese troops. Since Japanese ground forces could not assault the vessels effectively, naval air units were requested to make the attack. The supreme naval commander, Vice-Admiral Kiyoshi Hasegawa, was well aware of the potential dangers involved in violating the rights of nonbelligerents in China and correspondingly imposed many restrictions on bombing or strafing any vessel in the Yangtze River. Indeed, the Japanese naval commander had been consistently informed as to the whereabouts of foreign vessels and the information was subsequently forwarded to the subordinate commands throughout the area. As early as December 11, Yarnell had given Hasegawa a running account of the *Panay's* exact positions in the Yangtze, but since army intelligence specifically verified the target as Chinese, a strike was ordered by Lieutenant Commander Kurio Toibana, the air operations officer. Prior to issuing the attack order, Toibana had been notified that the *Panay* was moving to a new location on the fateful morning to escape bombardment from Japanese shore batteries but Toibana ignored the announcement until the gunboat's position was confirmed by the Japanese consulate in Shanghai. Certain that the intelligence report was accurate and certain that the pilots making the strike would not blunder into attacking neutral vessels, he then proceeded with the order. Not until 5 p.m. did Toibana learn that the *Panay's* location was ominously similar to the position given by army intelligence of the alleged Chinese vessels. By then, it was too late.[10]

The Japanese attack force, consisting of nine fighters and six dive bombers from the Twelfth Air Group and three bombers and six dive bombers from the Thirteenth Group, reached their target in V-formation at 1:37 p.m. on December 12. Without warning, a wave of three twin-engine bombers attacked in succession from out of the sun at an altitude of not more than 1000 feet. The first shells struck the port bow, snapped the foremast and destroyed the forward three-inch gun. Other direct hits wrecked the pilot house, sick bay, radio room and wounded the vessel's captain. The first wave also concentrated their attack on the *SS Meian,* scoring at least three direct hits which left her burning and disabled. During the second attack, three of the *Panay's* .30 caliber machine guns were manned and fired but inflicted little damage since the planes came from the direction of the sun and made visibility difficult. In the succeeding waves, six fighters began to machine-gun the vessel while the bombers continued their devastating onslaught. In the next 25 minutes, 20 bombs were dropped on or near the helpless vessel and by 2:05 p.m. the gunboat began to list to the starboard; as the portable pumps were broken and the boiler was smashed there was little hope of pumping the water out of the vessel or of beaching her.[11]

While the *Panay* remained helpless, the Japanese concentrated all their attacks upon the oil tankers. The *Meian,* badly damaged from the first wave, was beached and its commander, Captain Carlson, killed. The *Meiping* and *Meihsia,* slightly damaged during the initial attacks, were beached along the left bank down river from the *Panay*. Both vessels then attempted to escape further attacks by proceeding to the right bank and anchoring at Kaiyian wharf. By 2:25 p.m. they had been destroyed by succeeding waves of dive bombers.[12]

With her power and propulsion lost, all hope was now gone of saving the *Panay* and Hughes issued orders at 2:05 p.m. to abandon the slowly sinking vessel. Two motor sampans were used to transport the survivors in three shifts to the north shore. While the first survivors were being taken ashore, one of the sampans with several wounded aboard was fired upon by two of the attacking planes—the first attempted to bomb it, the second machine-gunned the lifeboat. No one was killed in the process, though several were wounded by the attack. According to eye witness reports filed with Admiral Leahy and later confirmed by film, after the remaining survivors had reached shore, several Japanese planes repeatedly flew over the area with the apparent intention of exterminating them, but the dense reeds along the shoreline enabled the survivors to escape detection from the air.[13]

By 3 p.m. the last of the survivors had abandoned the gun-boat which was now settling by the starboard bow. Shortly thereafter, two Japanese armed patrol boats approached from the same direction as the launch which had visited the *Panay* a few hours earlier and began machine-gunning the damaged American vessel. Several Japanese soldiers boarded the gunboat on the port side, examined the vessel for several minutes and then departed. During the entire search, the American flags were still flying and in plain view of the Japanese party. The Japanese boats also patrolled the area where they believed the survivors had landed, but the reeds served as an effective camouflage and the patrol abandoned the search. By 3:54 p.m., battered by over two dozen direct hits and near misses, the American flags still visible, the *Panay* rolled over and sank at the lower entrance of Hoshien Channel in ten fathoms of water. Killed in the attack were Charles Ensminger, Edgar Hulsebus, both seamen, and Sandro Sandi, a prominent Italian correspondent. Twelve men were seriously wounded, including J. Hall Paxton, second secretary to the American Legation in Nanking, while 38 were less seriously wounded.[14]

After dark, the survivors managed to reach several farm houses in relays one mile inland and there they obtained food and temporary shelter. Improvised stretchers for the wounded were constructed and the survivors proceeded to Hoshien, five miles distant and three miles inland. From Hoshien, Atcheson telephoned American medical missionaries at Anking and Luchowfu for aid and also asked them to relay what had occurred to the appropriate American military officials in Shanghai and the American ambassador in Hankow. The threat of another Japanese attack in Hoshien forced the survivors to journey in six borrowed junks on the following evening to Hanshan, 20 miles inland with the object of proceeding to Luchowfu, there to leave the wounded at the American missionary hospital while the fit would proceed to Hankow. Meanwhile, American, British and Japanese officials had learned of the incident and immediately dispatched vessels to rescue the survivors. On the morning of December 14, Admiral Holt of the British Navy informed Atcheson by telephone that help had arrived at Hoshien. The survivors journeyed back to Hoshien where they were met that evening by the *USS Oahu*, dispatched from Kaikuing, along with the *HMS Bee, HMS Ladybird*, the Japanese gunboat *Hodzu*, two Japanese destroyers and a seaplane. The *Oahu, Labybird* and *Hodzu* took many of the survivors and proceeded to Shanghai while the *Bee* transported the badly wounded survivors to Wuhu.[15]

The American vessel had been sunk by naval air units acting under intelligence reports by the army. When Hasegawa learned of the tragedy, he immediately offered his resignation, though he had no direct responsibility for the act. Hasegawa's resignation was refused by the Japanese government, but Admiral Teizo Mitsunami, commanding the Second Combined Naval Air Group, was removed from his post and re-assigned elsewhere. Indeed, the Japanese Naval Minister, Mitsumasa Yonai, reprimanded the commanders of the air groups making the actual attack, although the reprimand was mild since Yonai vainly attempted to whitewash the navy's sole responsibility for the entire affair:

> . . . your actions in attacking American vessels on the Yangtze River 12 December 1937, without definitely identifying your target, is deemed a failure in the performance of your duties. You will henceforth exercise greater care.

The Japanese Navy in general believed that army officers involved in the incident senselessly displayed poor judgment in disregarding international law by their order to machine-gun the stricken vessel. The navy felt that the failure to report this matter to higher authorities not only made matters worse but aggravated the confusion immediately following the sinking. Moreover, it was felt that American ill-will toward Japan was further heightened by Hashimoto's needless shelling of neutral vessels on the Yangtze River. The naval command believed that the incident could have been resolved more readily if the army had not been involved.[16]

The army command, by contrast, not only treated the crisis as an insignificant matter but an unfortunate accident which occurs in a war where neutrals are present in the area of hostilities. Upon learning of the sinking and the subsequent machine-gunning of the vessel and its lifeboats, army officials quickly offered several alibis:

> 1. That no Japanese patrol boats were in the area during the attack.

2. That the American gunboat provoked the incident by firing upon Japanese troops with her main guns (though they failed to explain how the vessel's three-inch guns remained covered by canvas when she sank).

3. That Japanese patrol boats never really fired on the *Panay*.[17]

Even Grew hesitated to believe the initial reports that a Japanese patrol boat could have machine-gunned and later boarded the *Panay*, since available information indicated that Japanese vessels did not reach Nanking until December 13. The American ambassador further believed that from a military point of view such an attack would have required a prearranged plan to coordinate an air-ground assault. Such a plan, according to Grew, was out of the question, for the Japanese Navy worked independently of the army even from the beginning of hostilities in July.[18]

News of the sinking electrified the United States on the morning of December 13, and in some quarters demands were now made to intervene directly in the Far Eastern conflict. Though many newspapers supported a stronger policy toward Japan, editorial reaction to the incident was surprisingly mild. Indeed, there developed a growing insistence that American nationals and naval contingents be completely withdrawn from China. Typical of this editorial expression was the *Portland Oregonian* which viewed the sinking as unfortunate but questioned the validity of the vessel being in such a critical area. "The United States government," the editorial declared, "should address a sharp note of protest to itself for having permitted the gunboat to be in that exposed position." The *St. Louis Post-Dispatch* adopted a similar position when it candidly asserted that "American military forces must be withdrawn from the Japanese-Chinese battle zone." The editorial writer believed that it would be sheer folly for the United States to risk the lives of American military forces merely to defend the few Americans who decided to remain in the war zone. The *Post-Dispatch* predicted that the sinking was an ominous warning to the United States to withdraw from China. "Protest to Japan and obtain compensation but remove our forces."[19]

The *Nashville Banner* considered the attack as deplorable but not surprising as long as the United States continued to station such vessels in a war zone. "Why should American vessels and troops," the editorial asked, "be left in the waters that are daily being churned by the bombs of combatants?" The editorial further questioned the Administration's intention of advocating peace when it declared:

> The idea of a number of American gunboats being scattered
> along the Yangtze River for a distance of 25 miles, in an area that
> is daily being bombed or threatened from the air is a strange
> procedure, if the United States really wants peace.[20]

The *Albuquerque Journal* made its views evident when it asserted that "the majority of citizens do not favor endangering
the peace of this country by incidents that may arise as a result
of our efforts to protect property rights in China. They would
prefer complete withdrawal." The *Louisville Times,* on the other
hand, took a cautious viewpoint over the sinking and felt that
the American people should not make war demands similar to
those which had occurred over the *Maine* incident. The editorial
believed that the tragedy "was not the result of malice upon the
part of the Japanese government toward Americans."[21]

The *Cincinnati Inquirer* viewed the sinking with a mixed attitude of isolationism and condemnation. On the one hand, the
editorial asserted that the killing of a few Americans did not
justify a war which might result in the death of thousands of
Americans and the ruin of the economy. The *Inquirer,* moreover,
pointed out that the American claims and interests in China were
relatively weak. "Had the United States identified fully with the
other powers in 1931 and maintained a united policy toward the
Far East, our position today would not be nearly as inaffective as
it is."[22]

The *Philadelphia Inquirer* cautioned the nation and the President to refrain from taking a jingoistic view "in a situation which
is fraught with volcanic potentialities." As the crisis developed
diplomatically, the *Inquirer* expressed the opinion that nothing
would be gained by remaining in China:

> Continued maintenance of our naval forces in China can serve
> no good and after all our nationals have been evacuated. Continu-
> ance of our gunboats in Chinese waters is a constant threat to our
> involvement in war and . . . we have no concernably sane excuse
> to get mixed up in this Asiatic war. It is Japan's war. It is China's
> war. It is not our war.[23]

The *Detroit Free Press* also remained hesitant and warned
against any hasty judgment of action by the United States, particularly so since Japan desired a peaceful settlement of the crisis.
"The Tokyo government," the editorial added, "generally has
respected America, has desired its friendship and has been scrupu-
lous in honoring its engagements and keeping its promise with
the United States." The editorial concluded by presuming that

the Japanese assurances and expressions of regret were sincere and dependable.[24]

In an editorial, the *Christian Science Monitor* did not view the *Panay* crisis as another *Maine* or *Lusitania* incident in its intensity but maintained that the "present firm course of American diplomacy may well be wiser than a retirement under threats." In discussing the possibility of undertaking some form of collective action against Japan, the editorial writer saw little hope of such a move since the Brussels Conference had proven that little, if any, collective action among the Western powers could be initiated to stop Japan.[25]

The *Minneapolis Tribune* cautioned the people, in an editorial, to reserve judgment on the crisis. "The prelude to war," the editorial maintained, "is almost invariably a blind emotionalism which believes only what it wishes to believe and is utterly intolerant of the reasoned factual approach to any crisis."[26]

Several other newspapers took a fervent stand for withdrawal and opposed vigorously any demands for war over the incident. Such conservative newspapers included the *Richmond* (Va.) *Times-Dispatch* which strongly urged American withdrawal from China. "The blowing up of the gunboat *Panay*," the editorial remarked, "is just what we said was going to happen if this country persisted in keeping fighting ships in the Far Eastern danger zone." The *Times-Dispatch* pointed out that American nationals had been warned to leave China and should not demand protection at the risk of entangling the United States in war. An *Arizona Republican* editorial also demanded complete withdrawal from China and added caustically that "American business should not be allowed to become a vehicle to carry the nation into war." The *Birmingham News* reiterated this expression by maintaining that neutral vessels should remain out of war zones and warning against fostering a jingoistic attitude which might influence the Administration in adopting a premature decision over the crisis. The *Los Angeles Times,* which supported an American withdrawal from China, asserted candidly that "the general public will do well not to rock the boat and let the American State Department handle the matter without amateur assistance or interference."[27]

Several newspapers, however, adopted a middle of the road attitude over the sinking, advocating neither complete withdrawal from China nor a declaration of war. The *Little Rock Gazette* believed that the sinking would be a blow to American prestige in the Orient. The *Dallas News* advocated a wait and see policy while the *Burlington (Vt.) Free Press* indicated that nations having an interest in international trade should have impressed upon Japan that international law still existed; that no nation could continue to violate these laws and still rely upon the good will of neutral nations. The *Cleveland Plain Dealer* expressed the opinion that the United States was not seeking to become involved in the war but "we must not close our eyes to the fact that the world contains people less peace-minded than ourselves." This attitude was also emphasized by the *Indianapolis Star,* which pointed out that the United States was not a warlike nation; "we should, however, stand up for our rights and insist that they be respected." The *Boston Herald* firmly believed that American retaliation would be forthcoming if similar incidents should occur in the future. The editorial writer, however, felt that boycotting Japanese goods in the United States would be more effective and more damaging to Japan.[28]

Two isolationist journals insisted emphatically that the United States withdraw its nationals and armed forces from China before a more serious incident occurred. In an article in the *New Republic,* John T. Flynn questioned the convoying of Standard Oil vessels by an American warship when the former had been ordered out of the zone of hostilities. Indeed, Flynn condemned Roosevelt's foreign policy in China and warned that the Administration would ultimately embroil the nation in war with Japan. An editorial in the *Christian Century* stated that the Yangtze Patrol was merely a relic of nineteenth century imperialism and therefore should be eliminated. The journal expressed doubt whether Japan deliberately intended to entangle the two nations in a conflict over the incident. "It is incredible," the editorial maintained, "that the Japanese should have tried to arouse American belligerence by sinking this gunboat when they have obtained all they wanted from this country by the refusal of the President to invoke the neutrality laws."[29]

Various peace organizations flooded the President with urgent requests to withdraw American forces completely from the Orient; they advocated sending no reinforcements. The Peace Fellowship Society of Minnesota, the Syracuse Peace Council and the Woman's International League for Peace and Freedom all favored a settlement by peaceful means only, while the latter warned Roosevelt that "the incident of the *Lusitania* and the cry of the American people which followed that disaster may be repeated if America does not act at once." The Committee for Concerted Peace

Efforts declared that American indignation over the sinking was justified but warned against the adoption of extreme nationalism. The committee favored some form of world cooperation which would insist upon the sanctity of treaties as the answer to any future incidents. A Gallup Poll taken in January, 1938, further strengthened the isolationist attitude when 70 percent indicated they favored a complete withdrawal from China.[30]

Although the movement to remove American forces and nationals from the Far East received wide support, not all newspapers favored such a withdrawal. Some even advocated an end to America's isolationist policy. In an editorial, the *Newark Evening News* found it difficult to comprehend that the sinking was accidental and urged the government to remain steadfast and not withdraw its interests and protection to Americans residing in China. "If the United States is firm," the editorial asserted, "perhaps the need for a much larger degree of firmness will be averted in the not immeasurable future." The *San Francisco Chronicle* also believed that the United States should continue to maintain its forces in China "since a move of this nature would not entitle the United States to rights and respect anywhere by anybody." The *Chronicle* admonished the Japanese for failing to realize foreign vessels were in the Nanking area.[31]

The *Seattle Daily Times* asserted that American withdrawal of protection to its citizens, as isolationists were demanding, would weaken American moral and diplomatic influence in the Far East. The editorial further criticized isolationists in their attempts to influence the Administration since "such a sentiment against firm action is being built up that Roosevelt cannot possibly embark on any policy of economic sanctions or embargoes against Japanese goods. . . ." The *Rocky Mountain News* maintained that the American neutrality laws were partly to blame for provoking the sinking. "By our neutrality act," the editorial declared, "we led all the potential outlaw states to understand that we were not interested in what they did, so long as they refrained from attacking our shores." The editorial bitterly condemned isolationists who demanded a withdrawal from the Far East and asserted that "if we have no business in China, then our entire foreign policy . . . has been wrong since George Washington and we should begin now to revise it."[32]

Normally anti-Roosevelt in character, the conservative *Chicago Tribune* sanctioned the validity of the *Panay* being stationed in Chinese waters and whitewashed American responsibility by declar-

ing that "the United States did not intrigue to bring about the
trouble." The more out-spoken *Chicago Daily News* denounced
the Japanese rigorously for the unprovoked act and advocated a
firm if not warlike stand against Japan. Perceiving a future conflict between the two nations, the editorial warned ominously that
"every backward step, every withdrawal, every surrender, only
brings the eventual point of conflict that much nearer to our own
shores. We strongly urge that the Administration pursue the
strongest possible measures to convince the Japanese of their error."
In a letter to Hull, Colonel Frank Knox, publisher of the *Daily
News,* informed the secretary of state that the *Panay* incident
would not have occurred if the Japanese had not believed that
an isolationist attitude was prevalent in this country; that the
United States would not fight under any circumstances. Knox
advocated that a strong show of naval force be made in conjunction with the British in the Far East in order to convince the
Japanese militarists of the Western intention to thwart further
aggression.

A similar attitude was taken by several other newspapers, including the *Indianapolis Star,* which condemned the Japanese for
the sinking and maintained that the apologies which were offered
were "cheap and insincere." The editorial recommended that
strong measures such as economic pressure be instituted by the
United States government against Japan if American demands were
not met. The *Pittsburgh Post-Gazette* also insisted that harsh
measures be instituted against Japan so that she "be held accountable for this attack." The editorial maintained that Japanese
apologies or assurances could not absolve the destruction which
was caused and that future conflicts between the two countries
would merely bring "more bombing, more destruction and more
killing of American citizens." Supporting the same policy as the
Indianapolis Star, the *Post-Gazette* editorial advocated an economic
boycott against Japan.

In the nation's capital, the *Washington Post* criticized the
Japanese for the unprovoked attack and remarked caustically that
"it is a type of aggression for which statements of deep regrets
by smooth-tongued Japanese diplomats are totally inadequate."
The editorial also aimed its attack upon the isolationist groups
in the United States which accepted the apologies at face value
and warned Japan:

> . . . the Tokyo government should understand that our profes-
> sional pacifists are not representative of American public opinion

and that it would be highly dangerous for them to assume that Uncle Sam will swallow a long series of calculated affronts indefinitely.

The *Washington Evening Star* believed that the incident was merely the beginning of a systematic flouting of American rights in the Far East. "It is humiliatingly apparent," the editorial stated, "that Western prestige has suffered a severe if not an irretrievable blow."[35]

In the nation's largest city, the *New York Times* and the *New York Herald Tribune* each supported the stern attitude taken by the Administration; both newspapers favored Roosevelt's intention of keeping American naval forces in China. In an editorial, the former voiced the opinion that the attack must have been intentional and declared that "the State Department is fully justified therefore in the stern attitude it has taken." Writing for the *New York Herald Tribune,* columnist Walter Lippmann believed the prevention of such incidents in the future would be impossible if the President's actions in the *Panay* affair were not supported by Congress and the people. Lippmann upheld the government's conviction not to withdraw from the Orient since "there is no alternative but to insist firmly on nothing more and nothing less than our minimum . . . rights."[36]

Other newspapers throughout the country condemned the Japanese for the sinking and ostensibly took a grim view of the effect that the incident would have upon future Japanese-American relations. The *New Orleans Times-Picayune,* however, did feel that the government's firm protests would have an influence upon the Japanese in their future treatment of Americans in China, though it cautioned that Japan might be lulled into a false sense of security if the United States and other Western nations were not stirred from their inaction. A *Providence Journal* editorial predicted that Japanese-American relations would be "injured beyond all calculations" if a strong stand were not taken immediately, while the *Sacramento Union* recommended strict measures so that "Japan will see to it that we have no further provocations that might lead to war." The *Buffalo Evening News* declared that the United States should not permit such attacks to continue and advised a show of firmness as the only method of obtaining satisfactory results in the *Panay* affair. The *Boston Globe, Omaha World Herald* and the *Atlanta Journal* all favor the retention of American forces in the Far East and issued a warning to Japan to cease her attacks or, as the *Globe* editorial maintained, "face total commercial ostracism through the invocation and swift expansion of the provisions of the Neutrality Act."[37]

While requests were sent to Roosevelt advising American withdrawal, the President also received numerous telegrams from private citizens urging the use of severe measures against Japan. Indeed, an attitude that the national pride and prestige had been offended gripped the nation and, as one irate citizen explained, "when the American flag is trampled underfoot by responsible foreign officials and American blood spilled with impunity . . . righteous indignation should impel America to action." The Tennessee Veterans of Foreign Wars even went so far as to advocate war against Japan to avenge the sinking. Many Americans, on the other hand, now favored the concept of quarantining aggressor powers which the President had expressed in Chicago two months earlier. It was believed that by this method subsequent incidents such as the *Panay* could be averted. This policy was reiterated by such organizations as the New York-based American Friends of the Chinese People, which declared:

> This latest in the series of wanton acts of aggression by the military-fascist government in Japan is simply further proof of your statement in Chicago that the only path to peace is to quarantine the aggressor nations.[38]

American Communists also affirmed their support for such a policy, although with some modifications. Questioned as to whether they would support the Roosevelt Administration if war occurred with Japan over the sinking, Earl Browder, General Secretary of the American Communist Party, publicly announced that "we would support the American government in such a war to the extent that its policies and methods contributed toward the national independence of China. . . ." Browder did not favor the use of military intervention camouflaged under the façade of collective security, but he declared that the Communist Party would offer its moral and economic support.[39]

Meanwhile, a movement to boycott Japanese-made products gained wide popularity throughout the country. The Committee for Boycott Against Japanese Aggression, headed by Robert D. Leigh, President of Bennington College, issued a call to more than 50 civic and peace organizations to institute a nation-wide boycott of all Japanese goods. The committee believed that the purchase of Japanese commodities had supported Japanese aggression in the Far East and therefore called upon Americans to cease buying such products. William Green, President of the American Federation of

Top: The *U.S.S. Panay* is shown here during her standardization trial off Woosung, China, in August, 1928. The gunboat looked much the same when she began her fatal trip up the Yangtze River on December 12, 1937. **Bottom left:** This picture shows that the American flag was flying when the planes attacked, although the Japanese claimed they thought they were bombing a Chinese target. **Bottom right:** The Japanese twin-engine bombers first attacked at 1:37 p.m.

All photographs in this section are reproduced by permission of the National Archives and the U.S. Naval Photographic Center.

Top: During the second attack, three of the *Panay's* .30 caliber machine guns were manned and fired but they inflicted little damage since the planes came from the direction of the sun and made visibility difficult. **Bottom:** Her sides pecked by shrapnel, the *Panay* begins to list.

Top: Survivors began to abandon the ship by 2:05 p.m. With the pumps and boiler smashed, there was little hope of pumping out the water or of beaching her. **Bottom:** Wounded passengers and crew members are helped into lifeboats.

Left: Crew members doff their shoes as they prepare to jump overboard and swim for shore. Top and Bottom: Survivors watched the listing and doomed *Panay* as the lifeboats carried them toward the safety of the shore.

Top left: With the *Panay* listing badly, a Japanese armed patrol boat pulls alongside and several soldiers board the gunboat, examine it for several minutes, and leave. **Top right:** Battered by over two dozen direct hits and near misses, the *Panay* rolls over and, **Left:** at 3:54 p.m., sinks at the lower entrance of Hoshien Channel in ten fathoms of water. **Bottom:** Survivors unload salvaged equipment on the Yangtze River's east shore.

Top: Boatswain's mate Mahlmann and Ensign Biwerse direct landing of medical supplies. **Bottom:** Bamboo thickets shield passengers and crew from continued shelling from planes and patrol boats as first aid is given to the wounded.

Top: Well-known Italian journalist Sandro Sandi is comforted by his colleague, Signor Barzini, just before he died. **Bottom:** The *Panay's* wounded captain, J. J. Hughes, lies among the reeds on the shore with a broken leg.

Top: Quartermaster John H. Lang, wounded during the first bombing attack, watches returning Japanese planes from his hiding place in the bamboo thickets. **Bottom:** After improvising stretchers for the wounded, the *Panay* survivors start inland to look for food and temporary shelter.

Labor, also called upon labor to initiate an economic boycott of Japanese goods. Green felt that adoption of this boycott would serve as an effective moral weapon which could be used by the American people in voicing their opposition to the *Panay* sinking.

Raymond L. Buell, President of the Foreign Policy Association, supported these moves with a plea for joint action to launch a "mass movement in every like-minded country" of a private boycott on Japanese goods. Buell announced a program which he believed would implement the effects of the movement:

1. American international agreement prohibiting loans to Japan.
2. Amendment of the Neutrality Act to give additional powers to the President to control exports and imports where belligerents are concerned.
3. Calling of a conference in Washington, D. C. on Far Eastern questions.

The association's program was never officially adopted by the government but its influence and the influence of other organizations did succeed somewhat in modifying purchases of Japanese commodities. Widespread boycotts which also included picketing of department stores selling Japanese goods, occurred from Boston to San Francisco and ultimately forced several stores such as the F. W. Woolworth Company to discontinue orders for these products.

Not all Americans, however, favored the principle of economic ostracism. Paul Homan of the Brookings Institute declared that any Anglo-American boycott "would only make Japan desperate and would move them to violence against American lives and property in China." Although he opposed any form of boycotts, Homan felt that a stiff attitude should be taken by the United States against Japan.[40]

Editorial opinion as expressed abroad in regard to the sinking varied from condemnation to praise to a pessimistic attitude that the incident was indeed a prophetic warning to the West of Japan's desire to dominate the Orient. This last sentiment was expounded particularly in England, where newspapers generally took a fateful view over the entire affair. Typifying this feeling was the *Manchester Guardian* which declared in an editorial that the bombing and sinking of American and British gunboats was merely a deliberate attempt on the part of Japan to expel the two Western nations from the Far East. "Japan will never be content," the editorial asserted, "to shake the rich old tree of China and allow her rivals to keep the fruit which falls." The editorial lauded the firm stand taken by the United States and earnestly hoped that cooperation between the two English-speaking nations would further improve "so that common action, whatever form it takes will be possible." The *London Observor* ostensibly analyzed the Japanese apologies as an attempt to prevent Anglo-American cooperation "by offering profuse satisfaction to the United States without giving equal satisfaction to Great Britain." Vigorously criticizing America's placid attitude in foreign affairs, *The Economist* (London) asserted that "Japan had now provided the American people with materials for a lightning course of self-education in international affairs." The editorial maintained that isolationism for the United States was a convenient but unattainable ideal.[41]

One of Britain's largest newspapers, *The Times* (London), bitterly denounced the Japanese for the *Panay* sinking and declared the affair as "an indelible stain on the honour of a Power whose armed forces once boasted a peerless tradition." The editorial pointed out that the United States had much to lose in the Pacific if the crisis were not settled favorable to American prestige and interests. *The Times* approved of British support in whatever action the United States would take in the Far East and categorically warned Japan that it would "not be far wrong if it attaches importance to the close Anglo-American cooperation surrounding the dispatch of both our protests."[42]

Editorial reaction in France took an attitude similar to the British newspapers and reviewed the episode as a threat to American prestige in China. The *Paris La Croix* believed that if the Japanese penetration into China were not stopped, Western interests there would be ruined. The *Paris L'Action Francaise* refused to accept the Japanese apologies that the sinking was the result of mistaken identity. "The Japanese government," the editorial remarked, "could not have been unaware that neutral vessels were in China and neither could their aviators." The editorial declared that Japan wanted to make it understood to the Western powers that non-belligerent gunboats were not welcome in Chinese waters. In an editorial, the *Paris Je Suis Partou* viewed the incident as a threat to French interests in Indo-China if the episode led to an outbreak of war between Japan and the United States and therefore called upon the Western democracies to contain Japanese aggression in the Far East.[43]

The two Fascist powers in Europe, although officially remaining neutral throughout the affair, nevertheless tended to sympathize with Japan by viewing the sinking as an accident that invariably occurs in time of war. In Germany, the *Volkischer Beobachter* displayed a pro-Japanese opinion when it declared that "true neutrality consists in the warships one leaves at home" while the *Borsen Zeitung* explained the accidental bombing as understandable when seen from a military point of view. Neither newspaper, however, mentioned the protests lodged by the United States. A similar opinion was expressed by Herman Goering's newspaper, the *Essen National Zeitung,* which dismissed the affair as "regrettable but in the history of military conflicts not uncommon."[44]

The *Berlin National Zeitung,* on the other hand, was more vehement in its attack upon the two democracies involved in the Yangtze crisis. According to the Berlin newspaper:

> The United States and Great Britain are endeavoring to turn an accident—a highly regrettable accident indeed, but one which has often occurred in the course of military history—into a big political event by attacks upon the Japanese government and army.

The pro-Japanese editorial writer declared that the Far Eastern conflict would not be decided by Western intervention.[45] The *Deutsche Allgemeine Zeitung* also justified the sinking when it maintained that Western gunboats should have expected to be fired upon after the vessels were warned repeatedly to withdraw from the zone of hostilities. "Rights which could not be enforced," the newspaper announced, "could hardly be said to exist."[46]

In Italy, American Ambassador Alfred N. Phillips, Jr. informed Hull that the Italian newspapers abstained from any editorial comment on the incident. Moreover, the Italian press not only refrained from reporting any eye-witness accounts but appeared to distort the facts surrounding the sinking and generally concluded in regard to the machine-gunning that several stray shots fired at Chinese troops probably struck the *Panay*. When the affair was settled ultimately, Mussolini's official newspaper, *Popolo d'Italia,* asserted caustically in an editorial that the United States settled the incident quickly since nothing specific could have been done to Japan. "They can only send notes," the newspaper editorial asserted, "to which Japan replied in a correct and solicitous manner which the government of the United States found satisfactory enough to liquidate the episode."[47]

Elsewhere in Europe, editorial opinion was generally critical of the Japanese for their unprovoked attack upon a neutral vessel. In Sweden, the conservative newspaper, *Nya Dagligt Allehanda* of Stockholm found it inconceivable that the Japanese government would attempt to incite a war with the United States. Criticizing the military authorities in their apparent outward contempt for the Western nations, the editorial declared:

> The Japanese Government, accordingly, will find it difficult to make the usual diplomatic considerations prevail and may be compelled to follow as far as possible the course set by the military authorities.[48]

The *Dagens Nyheter* of Stockholm, on the other hand, rigorously censored Japan's growing aggression in the Far East.

> America's prestige in the Far East has received a heavy blow and Japan has been able to prove in the most flagrant manner that the democratic states will acquiesce when threatened with unlimited brutality. Such a victory of force is from Japan's point of view worth any number of apologies . . .[49]

In Latvia, the *Riga Segodnya* openly condemned the machine-gunning of the sinking vessel by Japanese troops and branded the action as "unnatural and monstrous." According to the editorial, the Japanese could never justify the action as a mistake after committing such a violation of international law. "The infantry could not help seeing the American flag," the Latvian newspaper maintained, "so they had no need to fire and if they saw that the vessel was sinking they also had no right to fire because a fight is not an execution."[50]

According to John C. Wiley, the American Chargé d'Affaires in Austria, the incident produced a sensation in the Austrian press. The *Nevigheits-Weltblatt* of Vienna summed up Austrian reaction when it declared in an editorial that "the honor and the prestige of the United States are seriously injured." The editorial writer remarked that the United States had more to fear from the aggressive designs of Japan than their European counterparts, but the distance between the two countries would make it impossible for the Japanese to carry out any such plan. The Vienna newspaper maintained, however, that the sinking was deliberate on the part of the Japanese military and warned that "if it is Tokyo's aim to cut Europe and America off from the Asiatic East, then the latest incident on the Yangtze is not an isolated incident but an alarming warning."[51]

In Poland, the incident, according to North Winship, the American Chargé d'Affaires, was reported strictly as a news story without editorial comment. The Polish government, moreover, prohibited the showing of the Universal Pictures film of the sinking since "its viewing would endanger the good relations of Poland with a foreign country."[52]

Editorial reaction in Japan was, on the whole, highly toned with apologies and regrets, although a strict censorship of the press prevailed which left the Japanese public largely ignorant of the real attitude of the United States following the sinking. According to Grew, as late as December 21 the episode of machine-gunning the *Panay* and her survivors had been deliberately left out of the newspapers. Grew believed that the military leaders did not wish to disclose all the information regarding the incident to the press for fear that such knowledge might damage their influence domestically.[53]

The *Tokyo Asahi* was the only Japanese newspaper to report the incident when it occurred and in an editorial praised the continuing good relations between the United States and Japan. Although it deplored the sinking, the editorial categorically approved of the prompt expressions of regret and hoped that further measures would be taken in order to settle the misunder-standing as quickly as possible. "We are confident," the editorial declared, "that if Japan maintains an honest attitude a friendly nation will not fail to appreciate our sincerity."[70]

When the incident became known to other Japanese news-papers, more apologies and regrets quickly followed. The *Tokyo Nichi-Nichi* asserted that the entire affair was a mistake on the part of the Japanese naval planes and hoped that the United States and Great Britain would "not lose sight of their traditional calm and reason and will take due cognizance of our sincerity." The *Japan Times and Mail* maintained that the incident actually had improved relations between the two nations. The newspaper pointed to the widespread sympathy of the Japanese people as proof that relations with the United States were cordial. "The spontaneous good will shown by the Japanese people over the *Panay* incident," the editorial commented, "promises to set their old friendship on a deeper and firmer basis than ever before."

Only the *Tokyo Kokumin* took a grim and realistic approach to the sinking and in an editorial demanded that the veil of secrecy be lifted by the Japanese government concerning the entire affair.

> Of all the recent incidents there has not been any that has caused so much concern and unrest in the minds of the people as the *Panay* incident. What is the truth behind the *Panay* incident anyway? Why have we to offer apologies? What diplomatic negotiations have been going on between the government of Japan and the United

States? So long as this state of affairs exists, the government cannot hold the confidence of the people and solidify their convictions.[55]

In North America, Canadian editorial reaction not only showed a feeling of pessimism but also condemned Japanese aggression as well as Anglo-American complacency over the episode. Many Canadians believed that the Dominion would be vitally affected if war occurred over the incident. These consequences were reiterated by Ernest Lapointe, the Minister of Justice, when he declared in a speech in Quebec that due to "the present development of aerial combat, the Pacific and Atlantic coasts of Canada are in danger of attack in the event of either England or the United States becoming involved in war. . . ." The *Montreal Daily Star* asserted that the sinking would scarcely create a stir, let alone a war, and pointed out that if the United States and Great Britain intended to intervene in China, they would have done so earlier. A *Winnipeg Tribune* editorial, although deploring the Japanese attack upon the *Panay,* confirmed Canadian neutrality when it asserted that "there is no sentiment here for sending our young men to fight Japan in China." A similar but a more pessimistic attitude toward the conflict was taken by the *Winnipeg Free Press* when it maintained that the sinking would not be the last of its kind if Anglo-American forces remained in the Far East.

Several Canadian newspapers, however, castigated both the American and British governments for not assuming a more vigorous stand against Japan over the affair. The *Ottawa Journal* reminisced over how attitudes had changed, citing American revenge over the *Maine* disaster in 1898 and Viscount Palmerston's "Don Pacifico" speech in 1850 which asserted the rights of British citizens the world over.

> Remains too, the sting of the last war. The memory of those dead from Flanders to Picardy lives on; a terrible responsibility for those who would decree a world war. The pity of it is, and the loss, is that the dictators are profiting from the memory.[57]

In an editorial, the *Regina Leader Post* described vividly the placidity of the Western democracies in curbing Fascist aggression. "The Fascist nations," the editorial remarked, "have found the democratic nations quite adept in tactics suggestive of taking it on the chin and doing little or nothing about it in return." The *Toronto Globe and Mail* also asserted that Britain and the United States were being systematically stripped of their prestige in the Orient while the *Welland Tribune* avowed that if American jurisdiction were to be enforced in the Far East, stronger naval units should be dispatched to the area immediately. Without a powerful naval force, the editorial added, the United States "is merely inviting further Japanese interference by remaining in the war zone."[58]

Wesley Frost, the American Chargé d'Affaires in Chile, informed Hull that editorial reaction in Santiago criticized the general apathy of the United States and Great Britain over the incident. The *Santiago El Mercurio* believed that the failure of any joint action taken by the Anglo-Americans was the result of the latter's intention to maintain a policy of neutrality at any cost while the *El Imparacial,* ominously perceiving the rising tide of aggression in the world, warned the Western nations to mobilize in order to avoid potential disaster in the near future. With shocking clarity the leftist newspaper, *La Opinion* pointed out that the ineffective policies of the democratic countries enabled fascist nations to continue their acts of aggression with impunity and advised that a stronger attitude be adopted to halt wanton acts of destruction such as the *Panay* sinking.[59]

In Brazil, the *Rio de Janeiro O Jornal* took a more conciliatory position with regard to the Far Eastern incident and believed the sinking was quite accidental.

> It would be difficult to charge the Japanese with any deliberate purpose in the bombardment of the gunboat. It would have been a provocation contrary to policy which would not have been comfortable with any of the important national interests of the movement.[60]

In the United States, Congressional reaction paralleled that of the newspapers. News of the *Panay* disaster touched off a heated debate in Congress over the present policy in China, though a war spirit was curiously absent. Nor, for that matter, were there indications that such measures as sending additional naval units to the Far East were contemplated. On the contrary, a wave of isolationist sentiment swept through Congress demanding the withdrawal of all American nationals and armed forces from China. In the Senate, William E. Borah took the lead in opposing any firm action over the episode. Borah did not view the sinking as a threat to the national safety and therefore brushed aside proposals for sending an ultimatum to the Japanese government. "I am not prepared," he informed a constituent, "to vote to send our boys into the Orient because a boat was sunk which was traveling in a dangerous zone. That which happened might be expected to happen under such circumstances. War is war." Borah was certain that the United States could protect its nationals in

China without becoming involved in war and was confident that the nation's interests and self-respect could still be maintained by remaining aloof from the Sino-Japanese conflict.[61]

Other members of Congress supported these measures; they further advocated a complete withdrawal from the Orient or, at the very most, some form of economic boycott against Japanese-made products. In the House, debate raged over such a course, although several members opposed any withdrawal or the adoption of any economic sanctions and boycotts. Leading the fight for an isolationist program was Maury Maverick of Texas who informed the House that "we should learn that it is about time for us to mind our own business," while Hugh Maas of Minnesota viewed the sinking as "further evidence that we should get out of the Orient." Representatives David J. Lewis of Maryland and Bryan N. Scott of California both maintained that economic sanctions instead of outright war would be more effective against Japan and offered resolutions to this effect. "The aggression of Japan and her violations of international laws," they declared, "can be effectively met . . . by the method of economic sanctions." Stiff opposition for any enactment of sanctions, however, never removed that issue from the debating stage.[62]

Though generally an isolationist, in this instance Hamilton Fish, Jr., of New York supported the Administration's demand that Japan apologize, offer indemnities, and provide definite guarantees that such incidents and attacks upon American warships and citizens would not re-occur in the Far East. Indeed, Fish maintained a firm stand over the affair, although he believed that war with Japan over the sinking "would be criminal folly with nothing to gain and everything to lose." Fish did favor an eventual withdrawal of American naval units from the Far East but he felt that such a move should not occur during a time when an American gunboat had been sunk or in the face of threats. He advocated instead for the construction of a navy second to none as a means to check further attacks upon American naval forces. If the American Navy were larger and more efficient, according to Fish, Japan would have second thoughts about launching into a naval war with the United States.[63]

Fish opposed instituting commercial boycotts against Japan, since it might cause the destruction of America's Far Eastern trade, or at most, lead ultimately to war. In an interview with the press, he reiterated this viewpoint when he declared:

> If we adopt this provocative policy and permit it to spread—
> that we will not buy from Japan, that we will boycott her, that we

will go further into embargoes, reprisals and economic sanctions—then I say it is a step toward war.[64]

In place of adopting sanctions, Fish favored invoking the Third Neutrality Act in order to restrain Japanese aggression in the Far East. If this act were in effect, as Fish pointed out, Japan would be unable to procure raw materials freely or purchase any amounts of arms and ammunition in the United States.[65]

A similar debate occurred in the Senate, where isolationist forces attempted to issue the call for a withdrawal from China and the enactment of economic sanctions against Japan as measures to prevent war. Such isolationist senators as Robert R. Reynolds of North Carolina pursued this line of reasoning "because we are going to become involved in serious trouble and what the American people want is that we stay away from entanglements and embroilments and stay out of war." Reynolds feared that the Chinese might "accidentally" destroy American vessels there simply to draw the United States into a war with Japan. The North Carolina senator proposed a complete withdrawal; he remained indifferent to the loss of American prestige and investments in China that such moves would bring. Reynolds was supported by Senator Henry F. Ashurst of Arizona who favored any program which would avert the possibility of war with Japan rather than offer viable alternatives to the crisis, and by Senator Arthur Capper of Kansas who declared that "the gunboats on the Yangtze should be withdrawn as soon as possible to avoid further complication . . . we want no war with either Japan or China."[66]

Not all the senators, however, accepted these impassioned pleas for American withdrawal. Several members of the Senate fully realized the damaging effect the episode would have upon the nation's prestige and therefore attempted to undermine the allegations made by the isolationist factions. Hiram Johnson of California staunchly defended American rights in China and the principles involved, although he too hoped to avoid war if at all possible. He bluntly called for adequate protection for American nationals everywhere and refused to be bluffed out of this course, particularly by the tactics of the Japanese. "I will not subscribe," he told his colleagues, "to the idea that a gunboat of the United States may be blown to pieces because somebody may see fit to take a shot at her and then, subsequently with tongue in cheek, say that he is sorry and apologize." Elbert D. Thomas of Utah and Edward R. Burke of Nebraska both assented to Johnson's overtures as the only wise course for the United States to pursue, while Alban Barkley of Kentucky refused to consent to any withdrawal from China since the gunboats were stationed in the Yangtze River solely to protect American nationals who might be in jeopardy. Key Pittman, chairman of the Senate Foreign Relations Committee, considered the incident as an odious scheme by certain Japanese officers to force neutrals and their military units out of China. He felt that these headstrong officers justified the attack upon the *Panay* following the failure of Roosevelt's quarantine speech in October and the Brussels Conference seven weeks later.[67]

Like their counterparts in the House, many senators favored the adoption of some type of commercial boycott as the only effective means of containing Japanese expansion. Several members, however, vetoed measures of economic sanction, while Borah refused to acquiesce to such proposals. Even as early as October 7 the Idaho senator did not feel that a boycott of Japanese products would thwart Japanese aggression:

> I am not much impressed with the idea of boycotting Japanese goods . . . Japan buys much more from us than we buy from Japan so we would not be helping ourselves economically and we would be adding fuel to the flames.[68]

Commenting on proposals by isolationists who favored withdrawal of American interests from the Far East, Admiral Yarnell informed Paul V. McNutt, the High Commissioner to the Philippines, that the United States had traded in the Orient since it began as a nation and would continue to do so regardless of what alternatives recalcitrant congressmen pursued. "This is a fact we must face," he wrote, "and it seems to me they are entitled to some form of protection from our government."[69]

But the paralyzing fear of war still prevailed among the majority members of the Senate and on December 20 Frederick Steiner of Oregon proposed a resolution which requested Hull to transmit to Congress the following statistics:

> 1. The approximate number of American nationals residing in the Republic of China on or about August 9, 1936, the number after that date and the number now residing therein.
> 2. The approximate number of officers and enlisted personnel of our Army, Navy and Marine Corps now stationed in said Republic.
> 3. The approximate amount of American capital invested in said Republic and the names of the principal investors.[70]

In proposing such a resolution, Steiner hoped to make the records on the China situation official and to point out the futility of the American stake there. Hull effectively answered the Senate resolution on January 8, 1938, in a detailed letter to Vice President John Garner. As of August 9, 1936, Hull wrote, 10,350 American nationals were residing in China. When the outbreak of hostilities occurred in July, 1937, the number of Americans living in China had increased to 10,500 but by November 6, 4,600 were evacuated while approximately 6,000 still remained.

With regard to American military personnel in China, the secretary of state pointed out that 814 soldiers were stationed in Tientsien, 528 marines in Peking and 2,555 marines in Shanghai. Of the force in Shanghai, some 1,500 represented reinforcements dispatched the preceding August to cope with the problems resulting from the Sino-Japanese conflict. According to Hull, 129 officers and 1,671 sailors were listed on 13 American naval vessels which constituted a portion of the United States Asiatic Fleet based in Manila. The Asiatic Fleet, as a whole, consisted of 44 vessels and with the exception of the heavy cruiser *USS Augusta,* was composed of submarines, destroyers, and gunboats. Of this fleet, 13 were in Chinese waters and nine were gunboats exclusively on duty there.[71]

Hull pointed out that American investments in China totaled $132 million in addition to approximately $40 million of Chinese obligations in default since the First World War, between $25-$30 million worth of property owned by American nationals residing in China and some $40 million worth of real estate belonging to American missionary and charitable organizations. In a further break-down, Hull indicated that 353 different firms; 40 Protestant and nine Catholic societies; and ten educational, medical, and philanthropic groups had investments in the Chinese Republic.

According to Hull, United States armed forces were stationed in Peking and Tientsien in order to protect American nationals, and, if necessary, to assist in evacuation during periods of emergency. Military detachments had been maintained in Shanghai since 1927 to protect Americans residing in the International Settlement from possible disorders for which local authorities could provide no protection. Gunboats were stationed in Chinese waters also, for the express purpose of protecting American citizens there.[72]

Prior to the outbreak of the Sino-Japanese hostilities in July, 1937, the State Department had expected to withdraw American military units from China, but circumstances since July had caused a temporary interruption in these plans. Hull pointed out that American forces there had rendered invaluable service and assistance, not only in safeguarding and evacuating American nationals from the area of hostilities, but in helping to maintain diplomatic communications. He impressed upon the senators that:

> The interest and concern of the United States in the Far Eastern situation . . . are not measured by the number of American citizens residing in a particular country at a particular moment nor by the amount of investment of American citizens there nor by the volume of trade. There is a broader and much more fundamental interest— which is that orderly processes in international relationships be maintained.[73]

According to Hull the issues at hand extended beyond the negative achievements which many congressmen sought in the present crisis. The secretary of state believed that American influence in the end could assure peace in the Far East and the only effective way to remain out of war was to make certain that war did not occur. Trade with any nation, and the number of American citizens and the amount of property in any given country he felt would be irrelevant when compared with the prospects and potentialities of another world war.[74]

Congress continued to debate the issues of war and peace, isolationism and interventionism, boycotts and economic intercourse, but the enactment of any specific legislative program was held in abeyance by the lawmakers until a diplomatic settlement might be reached between the two countries.

Notes

[1] U.S., Department of State, *Foreign Relations of the United States, Japan 1931-1941* (Washington: GPO, 1943), pp. 517-518. Cited hereafter as *Foreign Relations, 1931-1941*.

[2] Joseph C. Grew, *Ten Years in Japan* (New York: Simon and Schuster Inc., 1944), p. 233.

[3] Letter of C. E. Gauss to S. Okamoto, December 10, 1937. "Correspondence Relating to the Sinking of the *USS Panay*," Naval History Division, National Archives, Record Group 45.

[4] *Foreign Relations, 1931-1941*, pp. 533-534.

[5] U.S., Department of State, *Foreign Relations of the United States, Diplomatic Papers, 1937* (Washington: GPO, 1954), III, 488. Cited hereafter as *Foreign Relations, 1937*; see also Irving S. Friedman, *British Relations With China, 1931-1939* (New York: Institute of Pacific Relations, 1940), pp. 102-103.

[6] Johnson to Hull, December 12, 1937. 394.115 Panay/350, National Archives, Record Group 59. Cited hereafter as NA, RG 59.

[7] *Foreign Relations, 1931-1941*, p. 534. The SS *Meihsia* anchored some five hundred feet ahead of the *Panay*, the SS *Meiping* about three hundred feet from the *Meihsia* on the latter's starboard quarter and the SS *Meian* about seven hundred feet behind the *Panay*.

[8] Kemp Tolley, "Yang-Pat—Shanghai to Chunking," *United States Naval Institute Proceedings*, 89 (June, 1963), 88.

[9] *Foreign Relations, 1931-1941*, p. 535.

[10] Masatake Okumiya, "How The *Panay* was Sunk," *United States Naval Institute Proceedings*, 79 (June, 1953), 591-592.

[11] *Ibid.*, p. 589; see also Universal Picture Film #506, Motion Picture Division, National Archives; *Foreign Relations, 1931-1941*, pp. 536-537; CINCAF to Navy Department, December 16, 1937, NA, RG 59; Tolley, p. 89; Samuel E. Morrison, *The Rising Sun in the Pacific* (Boston: Little, Brown and Co., 1950), III, 17.

[12] *Foreign Relations, 1931-1941*, p. 538.

[13] Leahy to Hull, December 16, 1937. 394.115 Panay/231 NA,RG 59.

[14] *Foreign Relations, 1931-1941*, p. 537; see also Tolley, p. 88.

[15] *Foreign Relations, 1931-1941*, pp. 538-539. See also CINCAP to Navy Department, December 14, 1937. 394.115 Panay/53, NA, RG 59.

[16] Okumiya, pp. 592, 596.

[17] Haldore Hanson, *Human Endeavor: The Story of the China War* (New York: Farrar and Rinehart, Inc., 1939), p. 147.

[18] *Foreign Relations, 1937*, p. 508.

[19] *Portland Oregonian*, December 14, 1937, p. 8; *St. Louis Post-Dispatch*, December 14, 1937, p. 20.

[20] *Nashville Banner*, December 14, 1937, p. 6.

[21] *Albuquerque Journal*, December 14, 1937, p. 8; *Louisville Times*, December 13, 1937, p. 4.

[22] *Cincinnati Inquirer*, December 16, 1937, p. 4.

[23] *Philadelphia Inquirer*, December 14, 1937, p. 12; December 18, 1937, p. 8.

[24] *Detroit Free Press*, December 17, 1937, p. 6.

[25] *Christian Science Monitor,* December 18, 1937, p. 14.

[26] *Minneapolis Tribune,* December 14, 1937, p. 14.

[27] *Richmond Times-Dispatch,* December 14, 1937, p. 12; *Arizona Republican,* December 15, 1937, p. 10; *Birmingham News,* December 13, 1937, p. 6; *Los Angeles Times,* December 14, 1937, p. 4.

[28] *Literary Digest,* January 8, 1938, p. 8.

[29] John T. Flynn, "Landon-Roosevelt War—Game Huddle." *New Republic,* January 8, 1938, pp. 254-255; *The Christian Century,* December 22, 1937, pp. 1582-1583.

[30] *USS Panay,* OF 150-C. Franklin D. Roosevelt Papers, The Franklin D. Roosevelt Library, Hyde Park, N. Y. Cited hereafter as Roosevelt Papers; Correspondence, December 15, 1937, Cordell Hull Papers, Manuscript Division, Library of Congress, Box 229. Cited hereafter as Hull Papers; George Gallup and Claude Robinson, "Public Opinion Survey, 1935-1938," *The Public Opinion Quarterly,* 2 (July, 1938), p. 389.

[31] *Newark Evening News,* December 15, 1937, p. 16; *San Francisco Chronicle,* December 14, 1937, p. 12.

[32] *Seattle Daily Times,* December 14, 1937, p. 6; *Rocky Mountain News,* December 15, 1937, p. 4.

[33] *Chicago Tribune,* December 17, 1937, p. 18; *Chicago Daily News,* December 14, 1937, p. 18; Correspondence, December 15, 1937, Hull Papers.

[34] *Indianapolis Star,* December 14, 1937, p. 18; *Pittsburgh Post-Gazette,* December 14, 1937, p. 1.

[35] *Washington Post,* December 15, 1937, p. 14; *Washington Evening Star,* December 15, 1937, p. 6.

[36] *New York Times,* December 19, 1937, p. 8; Walter Lippmann, "Today and Tomorrow," *New York Herald Tribune,* December 16, 1937, p. 12.

[37] *New Orleans Times-Picayune,* December 14, 1937, p. 8; *Providence Journal,* December 14, 1937, p. 10; *Sacramento Union,* December 17, 1937, p. 4; *Buffalo Evening News,* December 14, 1937, p. 22; *Boston Globe,* December 14, 1937, p. 16; *Omaha World Herald,* December 14, 1937, p. 10; *Atlanta Journal,* December 14, 1937, p. 12.

[38] *USS Panay,* OF 150-C. Roosevelt Papers.

[39] Earl Browder, *Fighting for Peace* (New York: International Publishers Co., 1939), p. 78.

[40] *Christian Science Monitor,* December 20, 1937, p. 1; *Washington Post,* December 17, 1937, p. 16.

[41] *Manchester Guardian,* December 14, 1937, p. 6; *The Economist* (London), January 1, 1938, p. 7; *London Observor,* December 19, 1937, p. 5.

[42] *The Times* (London), December 14, 1937, p. 17; December 16, 1937, p. 15.

[43] *Paris La Croix,* December 16, 1937, p. 5; *Paris L'Action Francaise,* December 14, 1937, p. 7; *Paris Je Suis Partout,* December 24, 1937, p. 4.

[44] Telegram from the American Ambassador in Germany to the Secretary of State, December 16, 1937. 394.115 Panay/174. NA, RG 59; *Literary Digest,* January 1, 1938, p. 11.

[45] *Manchester Guardian,* December 18, 1937, p. 15.

[46] *The Times* (London), January 17, 1937, p. 16.

[47] Telegram from the American Ambassador in Italy to the Secretary of State, December 21, 1937. 394.115 Panay/165, NA, RG 59; *New York Times,* December 28, 1937, p. 12.

[48] Telegram from the American Minister in Sweden to the Secretary of State, December 15, 1937. 394.115 Panay/222 NA, RG 59.

[49] *Ibid.,* January 3, 1938.

[50] Telegram from the American Chargé d'Affaires in Latvia to the Secretary of State, December 19, 1937. 394.115 Panay/295. NA, RG 59.

[51] Telegram from the American Chargé d'Affaires in Austria to the Secretary of State, December 19, 1937. 394.115 Panay/235. NA, RG 59.

[52] Telegram from the American Chargé d'Affaires in Poland to the Secretary of State, January 26, 1938. 394.115 Panay/354. NA, RG 59.

[53] Grew to Hull, December 21, 1937. 394.115 Panay/168. NA, RG 59.

[54] Grew to Hull, December 14, 1937. 394.115 Panay/67. NA, RG 59.

[55] *Tokyo Nichi-Nichi,* December 16, 1937, p. 8; *Japan Times and Mail,* December 22, 1937, p. 9; *Tokyo Kokumin,* December 20, 1937, p. 3.

[56] *Montreal Gazette,* December 20, 1937, p. 4; *Montreal Daily Star,* December 13, 1937, p. 6; *Winnipeg Tribune,* December 14, 1937, p. 7; *Winnipeg Free Press,* December 14, 1937, p. 5.

[57] *Ottawa Journal,* December 15, 1937, p. 5.

[58] *Regina Leader Post,* December 18, 1937, p. 11; *Welland Tribune,* December 16, 1937, p. 6.

[59] Telegram from the American Chargé d'Affaires in Chile to the Secretary of State, December 22, 1937. 394.115 Panay/213. NA, RG 59.

[60] Telegram from the Counselor of the American Embassy in Brazil to the Secretary of State, December 29, 1937. 394.115 Panay/263. NA, RG 59.

[61] Correspondence, December 17, 1937, William E. Borah Papers, Manuscript Division, Library of Congress. Cited hereafter as Borah Papers.

[62] *New York Times,* December 14, 1937, p. 18.

[63] *U.S. Congressional Record,* 75th Cong., 2nd Sess., 1937, LXXXII, Part 2, 1968.

[64] *Christian Science Monitor,* December 21, 1937, p. 2.

[65] *U.S. Congressional Record,* 75th Cong., 2nd Sess., 1937, LXXXII, Part 2, 1971-1972.

[66] *Ibid.,* p. 259; *New York Times,* December 18, 1937, p. 2.

[67] *U.S. Congressional Record,* 75th Cong., 2nd Sess., 1937, LXXXII, Part 2, 1357, 1911; *New York Times,* December 14, 1937, p. 18.

[68] Correspondence, October 7, 1937, Borah Papers.

[69] Yarnell to McNutt, January 1, 1938. Harry E. Yarnell Papers, Manuscript Division, Library of Congress. Cited hereafter as Yarnell Papers.

[70] U.S. Congress, Senate, *Resolution of Inquiry Relative to American Nationals, Armed Forces and Investments in China,* 75th Cong., 3rd Sess., 1938, p. 48.

[71] *U.S. Congressional Record,* 75th Cong., 3rd Sess., 1938, LXXXIII, Part 2, 261.

[72] *Ibid.*

[73] *Ibid.,* p. 262.

[74] Cordell Hull, *The Memoirs of Cordell Hull* (New York: The Macmillan Co., 1948), I, 567.

CHAPTER III

THE SETTLEMENT

When news of the sinking of the *Panay* reached Washington, Roosevelt and Hull felt certain that the Japanese military leaders had attempted to warn the United States of Japanese power and aims in the Far East. Both men were also convinced that the Japanese government should be held accountable for the sinking since it had supported the course pursued by its forces in China and had failed to check its military leaders there. The President and Hull realized, however, that the United States was unprepared at this point to institute an effective show of force which might compel the Japanese to respect international treaties and to withdraw from China. Isolationist sentiment still engulfed the nation and an attitude was also developing in which it was feared that this insult to the national honor might involve the United States in the Far Eastern conflict. Roosevelt and his secretary of state hoped to avoid any direct intervention in the Sino-Japanese struggle but they believed that a firm stand should now be taken over the incident if American prestige in the Orient were to be salvaged.[1]

Late in the evening of December 12, 1937, Hull instructed Grew to inform the Japanese foreign minister of the serious effects the incident would have upon American-Japanese relations. "Impress upon him," Hull wrote, "the gravity of the situation and the imperative need to take every precaution against further attacks on American vessels or personnel."[2] Early on December 13, Grew informed the secretary of state that Hirota, upon hearing of the sinking, immediately conveyed his government's profound apologies and that Admiral Hasegawa had accepted full responsibility for the disaster. In an unprecedented move, the Japanese navy and war ministers also sent similar expressions of regret to the United States Navy and the War Department. Admiral

Hasegawa personally admitted to Admiral Yarnell that naval
planes had bombed the *Panay* and the Japanese Navy was therefore
prepared to accept the fullest responsibility for the sinking. In
an official statement, Hasegawa declared:

> In the course of the Nanking operations a most unfortunate
> incident occurred when the United States warship alongside other
> vessels was sunk. This incident is a matter sincerely and most deeply
> to be regretted.[3]

Later that morning, Hull conferred with Roosevelt to determine
what steps were to be taken over the crisis. A vigorous attitude
was adopted. The President thereupon instructed the secretary
to inform the Japanese ambassador:

1. That the President is deeply shocked and concerned by the news
   of indiscriminate bombings of American and other non-Chinese
   vessels on the Yangtze and that he requests that the Emperor
   be so advised.
2. That all the facts are being assembled and will shortly be presented to the Japanese government.
3. That in the meantime, it is hoped the Japanese government will
   be considering definitely for presentation to this government:
   a. Full expressions of regret and proffer of full compensation
   b. Methods guaranteeing against a repetition of any similar
      attack in the future.[4]

In a meeting between Hull and the Japanese ambassador that
afternoon, Saito offered his government's sincere apologies and
regrets and declared that the sinking was entirely the result of
mistaken identity. Japanese officials, Saito told Hull, had received
reports of Chinese troops fleeing the Nanking area by boat prior to
December 12, and in their haste to check this retreat, erred into
believing that the *Panay* was a Chinese vessel. The Japanese representative admitted that Tokyo had known of the whereabouts of
the *Panay* beforehand and therefore the bombing was nothing more
than "a very grave blunder." Hull then read Roosevelt's memorandum to Saito and added that a full investigation of the sinking
would be conducted and that the Japanese government would be
informed of its findings.[5] Hull immediately informed Grew of
Roosevelt's memorandum to Saito and instructed the ambassador
to inform Hirota that the vessels which were attacked and sunk on
the Yangtze had been there by treaty right; that American flags
were visible and that they were conveying Americans and other
neutral personnel away from the war zone. Moreover, the *Panay*
and the Standard Oil vessels consistently changed their position
several times to avoid any danger of being attacked accidentally.

The secretary further reiterated to Grew the consistent violations by the Japanese of neutral rights in China since the outbreak of hostilities and the failure of the Japanese government to assure non-belligerents that its armed forces would fully respect the rights and interests of these powers. Japanese forces, Hull wrote, had repeatedly violated these rights and the sinking of the *Panay* was uncontested proof of this violation.[6]

When Hull's note was related to Hirota, the Japanese minister remarked that Japanese forces were ordered to fire upon all vessels on the Yangtze during this critical stage of the campaign. As Saito had explained the episode, he informed Grew that Japanese planes were pursuing Chinese troops fleeing the Nanking area when they spotted the *Panay* some 26 miles above the Chinese capital. Since visibility was poor, the planes could not identify the nationality of the vessel even at a low altitude. The bombers attacked, he told the American ambassador, what they believed were vessels transporting Chinese troops fleeing the besieged city. Hirota emphasized this point and reiterated that the Japanese government would make full indemnification for all losses sustained and those responsible for the attack would be punished. Meanwhile, a cease fire had been ordered in the area so that the *Panay's* survivors could be safely transported out of the war zone. In reply, Grew pointed out to Hirota that the Japanese bombing operations in the Nanking area were apparently carried out without any concern against the possibility of attacking neutral vessels. As Saito admitted, the Japanese authorities in Tokyo and Shanghai had definite and prior knowledge that the *Panay* and its convoy were in the vicinity of hostilities. The American ambassador recounted the failure of the Japanese government to safeguard American nationals and property even after the Japanese had pledged repeatedly that such measures would be taken. Grew sought definite assurances from Hirota that American nationals, interests, and property in China would not be subjected to attack by Japanese forces in the future. The Japanese minister promised Grew that he would "do everything in my power to maintain good relations with the United States."[7]

Though Hirota had assured Grew that the Japanese forces in the Hoshien area would halt operations, Nelson T. Johnson, the American Ambassador to China, indicated to Hull that the *Panay's* survivors were in jeopardy as a result of continuous fighting there. Hull again urgently requested Grew, along with the British ambassador, to insist that the Japanese military forces halt their operations in the vicinity of Hoshien until the survivors were removed from the area. This request was complied with and the Japanese counsel-general at Shanghai informed Gauss that a temporary truce had been ordered in and around Hoshien until rescue operations were completed and while medical supplies were ordered to the area.[8]

Following the bombing and sinking of the *Panay*, the chief of naval operations believed that the American Pacific Fleet, in a show of determination, should have immediately blockaded Japan in a move which he felt would impress upon the Japanese the intentions of the United States to protect its vessels and nationals. At the very least, Leahy advocated that the fleet be mobilized for possible action in Asia while at the same time an agreement might be reached with Great Britain for a joint naval demonstration in the Far East. Conferring with Roosevelt and Hull, Leahy emphasized the need for preparing the fleet for such an undertaking but both the President and the secretary of state were cool to the plan since they were convinced that Congress would heartily disapprove of such a move as tantamount to war.[9]

The British also were vitally concerned and somewhat involved as a result of the events of December 12. A few hours prior to the bombing of the *Panay*, Japanese artillery batteries under Colonel Kingoro Hashimoto had attacked several British vessels, including the gunboat *HMS Ladybird* in which one seaman was killed and several others were wounded. Certain that the attack upon the British vessels had been deliberate on the part of the Japanese, both Chamberlain and Eden hoped that they would be consulted by the United States before any action was taken. The British leaders believed that the protests lodged by the American government over the *Panay* would have a greater effect and significance upon the Japanese government if such action were synchronized with British protests. In other words, the prime minister and his foreign secretary sought joint action instead of parallel action over the incidents.[10]

This policy was reiterated to the State Department by the British Ambassador, Sir Ronald Lindsay, on December 13. In a conversation with Sumner Welles, the American Under-Secretary of State, Lindsay declared that his government viewed both attacks as intentional, "though those in higher authority will presumably go through all procedure of diplomatic apology." He told Welles that the British would agree to hold secret military consultations with the United States as a further indication that his government would cooperate to curb such incidents as the *Panay* and *Ladybird* episodes in the future. In a later conversation with Welles, the British ambassador asserted that the recent events in China unfortunately had caused a loss of British prestige in Europe. Several nations were now wondering whether Great Britain would support them in the event of a general European crisis. "They feel," he declared, "that England appears to be unable to cope with the outrages committed against her own nationals and national interests in the Far East." Lindsay predicted, however, that public opinion would favor an Anglo-American show of force against Japan.[11]

Eden reinforced this belief when he told members of the House of Commons that if the United States increased their fleet in the Far East, the Chamberlain government under such circumstances might increase the British naval contingents there. He believed that neither country alone could offer a showing impressive enough to keep the Japanese from assaulting non-belligerents in China. The foreign secretary also added that the Foreign Office was conferring with France and the Netherlands regarding cooperative measures in protecting Hong Kong, French Indo-China, and the Dutch East Indies from possible Japanese aggression in these areas.[12]

All thought of a joint Anglo-American protest or a naval demonstration was ruled out by Roosevelt and Hull who favored parallel action instead. Roosevelt preferred to act independently of the British out of deference to the isolationist sentiment in the United States while the State Department believed that joint action at the present time would be inconsistent with the Nine Power Treaty. Moreover, it was believed that if a clash were to occur in the Far East, the burden of defending European possessions there would fall upon the United States, not Great Britain. The Administration felt that the British were too absorbed in European affairs to pursue any intensive naval buildup in the Orient. Even several British naval experts hesitated to reinforce their navy in Asia since only two battleships could be spared from the fleet in Europe. Such a move, they thought, would hardly impress the Japanese with British strength.[13]

The French government generally remained neutral throughout the Sino-Japanese conflict although in principle it approved of upholding the territorial integrity and the open door in China. French interests evolved around the Indo-Chinese area. When the Japanese penetrated farther into Central China, the French feared that the Japanese expansion might continue southward. The American ambassador in Paris indicated to Hull that various French statesmen were wondering what action the United States would now undertake in the Far East. They hoped that strong measures would be pursued by the United States against the Japanese since France would be unable to apply any pressure due to their commitments in Europe. The French also feared, he told Hull, a British naval withdrawal from European waters in order to support the American measures in China over the *Panay* episode. They felt such withdrawal would leave France alone to check German and Italian aggression in Europe. This feeling was expressed effectively in an editorial from the *Echo de Paris* on December 15 when it asserted that "British forces should not be withdrawn from the principal task, which consists of holding in check the two totalitarian states which are our neighbors."[14]

The American ambassador informed the French government of Roosevelt's memorandum to the Japanese government. The French wholly supported the action taken by the United States over the affair and hoped that the subsequent apologies and promises for indemnification which were given by the Japanese would clear the way for a peaceful settlement of the incident. The French, however, still remained somewhat skeptical of Japanese assurances that international laws and treaties would be respected in the future. Indeed, the French regarded the Japanese aloofness from any form of international cooperation as one of the weak links in this system. For this reason, they hoped that the United States would now assume Western leadership in the Far East since the European situation had compelled both the French and the British to concentrate their efforts in Europe.[15]

Japan's anti-Comintern allies officially remained neutral during the crisis over the *Panay* affair, although Italy and Germany continued to expound a pro-Japanese attitude. Italy, for example, did not have any vital stake in China and therefore remained essentially indifferent to the Japanese expansion into China. Indeed, both nations signed a commercial agreement on December 30, 1937, which provided for most favored nation concessions in their respective spheres of interest, while Italy diplomatically recognized the Japanese conquest of Manchukuo by establishing a legation at Hsinking. Japanese-Italian solidarity was further cemented when Count Ciano, the Italian Foreign Minister, informed the American ambassador in Italy that his government would refrain from lodging a protest to Japan over the death of

Sandro Sandi, the prominent Fascist correspondent killed during the attack.[16]

Unofficially, however, the Italian authorities were deeply concerned over the American-Japanese dispute, fearing that the conflict might lead the United States to an alignment with Great Britain. Italy hoped that the United States would continue to remain isolationist and aloof from world affairs. In this respect, the anti-Comintern powers would be able to handle any territorial disputes that might arise while the British, French, and Russians could do very little to oppose such moves. But, if joint action by the Anglo-Saxon powers were to ensue in the Far East, France and Holland might offer their support and neither Italy or Germany would be able to counter this Western bloc. Hence, Italy was not overly pleased that the Eastern member of the pact was creating such potential troubles, for if an Anglo-American alliance occurred, it might establish a dangerous precedent for future action elsewhere, especially in Europe.[17]

German official opinion over the *Panay* episode was summarized effectively by their ambassador to the United States. In a note to the German Foreign Ministry, Ambassador Dieckhoff remarked that the majority of Americans were still opposed to any foreign entanglements and therefore would resist any plan pursued by the Roosevelt Administration that might actively involve the United States in war. He added prophetically, however, that "if the American people should be frightened out of their lethargy, the jump from isolationism to interventionism would not be too big for them." Dieckhoff further informed his government that agitation against Japan over the sinking was having an effect upon the American people but he maintained that for the time being the United States would continue to follow a passive foreign policy. The German ambassador predicted that if a successful settlement to the episode did not occur, "the United States Government, despite all resistance within the country, will abandon its present passivity."[18]

On December 15, Grew informed Hull that when news of the sinking became known in Japan, cash donations from Japanese citizens had been received in the embassy as an expression of their sorrow over the attack. Since the money was received anonymously and therefore could not readily be returned, Grew suggested that it be given to the American Red Cross in China. In answer to Grew's suggestion, Hull told the ambassador that neither the American government nor any of its nationals should receive any cash donations but noted the possibility that the money might be donated to financing something in Japan as testimony to the amicable feelings between the two peoples. Admiral Yarnell also informed Hull that he had been offered a large sum from sailors from the Japanese Third Fleet which he had refused on grounds that he had no authority to receive the money.[19]

Grew had also cabled Hull on December 15, that Captain Eijiro Kondo, senior aide to the navy minister and commander of the Japanese Yangtze Patrol, had expressed his superior's sincere apologies over the sinking and had informed the American naval attaché in Shanghai that instructions had already been dispatched to their military officials to refrain from attacking any area in China where Western vessels were present. Kondo added that these orders were to be followed even if it resulted in a failure to attack Chinese troops. The Japanese commander announced that a naval investigation was planned which he felt would clear the navy from any responsibility for the incident.[20] Earlier that day, Grew reported to the secretary of state that the director of the American bureau of the Japanese Foreign Office informed the British embassy that:

> The Japanese government . . . upon the completion of investigations, [will] deal appropriately with those responsible for the incidents and also that they are prepared to make the necessary indemnifications for the losses sustained by the British and Americans.[21]

While the State Department was seeking a satisfactory solution to the incident, Roosevelt was searching for some way to counter the possibility that the Japanese would not make full restitution over the affair. As early as December 14, he requested from his Secretary of Treasury, Henry Morgenthau, a financial report of Japanese assets in the United States and whether the President had the power to hold these assets against payment for the damage inflicted. Morgenthau informed the President on December 15 that Japan possessed approximately $72 million in short-term securities and between $55 million and $125 million in long-term notes in the United States, while Japanese real estate and other commodities were valued close to $50 million. The secretary of treasury estimated that the total amount ranged between $152 million and $247 million at the time but warned his superior that the Japanese government could convert this total to pounds sterling in a matter of hours if they so desired.[22]

As to the authority needed by the President to take possession of these assets, Morgenthau told Roosevelt that under the provisions of the Trading with the Enemy Act of 1933 he might declare a state of national emergency and could therefore issue a restraining order forbidding any monetary exchange transactions with other countries and, in this particular case, with Japan. According to Morgenthau, the executive decree could be issued as a preventive measure against the possibility of war and, consequently, would provide a basis for securing an indemnity as well as a guarantee against subsequent attacks in the future. Morgenthau further pointed out that if the Japanese government attempted to convert its assets to foreign currency, the President could issue another decree requiring all such conversions made subject to licensing by the United States government. The Administration could then delay issuing the licenses in an effort to thwart Japanese counter moves. Morgenthau maintained that the nation was prepared economically to be placed on a war footing; he saw no reason in waiting for the Japanese to attack another American vessel.

> For us to let them put their swords into our insides and sit there and take it and like it and not do anything about it is un-American and I think that we've got to begin to inch in on these boys . . . How long are we going to sit there and let these fellows kill American soldiers and sailors and sink our battleships?[23]

In a meeting, Roosevelt discussed with other members of his cabinet the 1933 Act and the wide range of powers such a statute would give the President to impose economic sanctions against Japan. Roosevelt believed these powers were extensive enough to authorize an embargo upon specific and critical commodities needed by Japan, such as cotton and oil. The President told his cabinet, however, that economic sanctions would be initiated only after he consulted and secured the cooperation of other democratic nations if, of course, such a plan was needed at all. In the case of cotton, southern farmers, he maintained, could be compensated financially by the government for their losses if such an embargo went into effect.

Writing about the events years later, Secretary of the Interior Harold L. Ickes believed that war with Japan was a forgone conclusion and now was the most opportune moment for war since Japan still depended vitally upon the West for raw materials. Though a professed pacifist, Ickes believed that "sooner or later the democracies of the world, if they are to survive, will have to join issue—armed issue—with the fascist nations." He further told the President:

> This will mean that America and Japan will be at war and if that ever is to happen, aren't we strategically in a better position now than we will be after Japan has strengthened her hand militarily and perhaps replenished her treasury with spoils of China? If we should strike now, could we not put Japan in her place at a smaller cost in life and treasure than might be possible at a time hereafter?[24]

This attitude was supported by Vice President John Garner and by Secretary of Navy Claude A. Swanson, who, like his chief of naval operations, sought a declaration of war or, at the very least, the reinforcement of the American Navy in Hawaii. Even Roosevelt, according to Ickes, seemed to feel that war might occur over the incident. Roosevelt felt that the attack on the American gunboat was initiated by three fundamental motives:

1. An arrogant assault upon the United States if allowed to go unrebuked, would impress the Chinese with the power and strength of Japan.
2. Japan hoped to make it uncomfortable for any Western power to remain in China.
3. Japan hoped to force all Westerners out of China.

The President pointed to Japan's conquest of Manchukuo in 1931-32 as a prime example where American non-recognition of that state resulted in the closing of the open door there. For the same reason, he felt that Japan would impose restrictive tariff regulations in areas of China which they had already conquered. Hence, the President was convinced that if military means did not fully impress upon the West to withdraw from China, Japan would do so through economic restrictions there. Roosevelt favored a similar policy to that which some of the members of his cabinet had advocated, but did not wish to settle the crisis by war.[25]

Secretary Hull conferred with Far Eastern experts Stanley Hornbeck, Norman Davis, Sumner Welles, R. W. Moore, and Admiral Leahy on the *Panay* affair. The general concensus indicated that nothing useful could be attained by conversations with Japan. Davis, Moore, and Leahy favored a demonstration of force but Hull vetoed the plan. Like Roosevelt, the secretary of state wanted to see whether the Japanese government would accept the American demands in full. Hull also expected further detailed information shortly from eye-witness accounts of the attack which he felt would determine more specifically what measures the United States would take.[26]

By December 15, the *Panay's* survivors had been rescued and they immediately forwarded their accounts of the attack to the State Department. From these reports, Hull learned that before the gunboat had sunk, two Japanese army motor launches converged on the vessel, machine-gunned it at point blank range, boarded the ship, and departed five minutes later in what Hull considered to be complete indifference to the nationality of the vessel, which was quite apparent. He further learned that while the survivors were attempting to escape to shore, Japanese naval planes bombed and strafed the life-boats. When the survivors had reached shore, the planes continued to search the area in what appeared as an attempt to eliminate eye-witnesses to the attack. On December 16, Hull instructed Grew to inform the Japanese government of these facts while he would meet with Saito to discuss this new information.[27]

In a meeting between the Japanese ambassador and the secretary of state on the following day, Saito denied emphatically that the *Panay* or any of its survivors were fired upon with machine guns from Japanese motorboats and insisted that no such craft had been in the vicinity on December 12. Hull, however, pointed to specific evidence as proof to the contrary while a Japanese Army spokesman, who remained anonymous, admitted to American officials in China that army units had crossed the Yangtze on December 11 in several types of craft in the near vicinity of the sinking. At this point, the secretary of state showed Saito the documentary reports which indicated that two such motor launches had not only fired on the gunboat but boarded it as well. Counter to his statement, Saito further informed Hull that Japanese military and naval officials did not receive notification of the vessel's location prior to the attack. The secretary of state again denied this and pointed to Saito's own admission of this fact four days earlier. Hull then asserted that it would appear unusual for the Japanese officials not to have known that the *Panay* had left Nanking and anchored upriver. The vessel's movements, as Hull pointed out, were given in advance and at all times both by the American Embassy in Nanking and on the *Panay* to the Japanese officials in Nanking, Shanghai, and Tokyo. Moreover, Japanese armed forces must have known that neutral vessels were in the vicinity since the order was given to fire on all neutral vessels on the Yangtze.[28] Hull's point that Japanese forces knew of the whereabouts of the gunboat was also verified by the American ambassador in China when he indicated in a cable to the secretary that at 10:09 a.m. on December 12 a patrol boat with 20 soldiers aboard and commanded by Lieutenant Yomura Kami halted the *Panay* halfway from her ultimate destination. The Japanese officer sought information as to the purpose and destination of the vessel and inquired whether Chinese troops had been sighted in the area. Hughes informed the lieutenant of the *Panay's* destination but could not disclose the location of any Chinese units.[29]

At the same time, Admiral Hasegawa also attempted to whitewash the navy's sole responsibility for the attack which was contrary to his admission made to Yarnell immediately following the bombing. On December 20, the Japanese admiral told Yarnell that from the beginning, he had opposed the army order to bomb all vessels on the Yangtze between Wuhu and Nanking but that his protests were ignored and the order was subsequently carried out. He and other high-ranking naval officials were not endeavoring to have the army admit publicly that it was their order which ultimately caused the incident. The American admiral then asked Hasegawa why Japanese naval planes, after having made over 50 attacks in the Nanking area since September, did not recognize the *Panay* and the nationality of other neutral vessels which had been in the vicinity during the entire time. The Japanese naval commander admitted that his aviators had bombed and machine-gunned the gunboat, although the strike had been ordered by the army. During the siege of Nanking, however, Hasegawa indicated that communications with the advanced forces were poor and the cause of some confusion. The pilots, he informed Yarnell, believed that the *Panay* and its convoy were Chinese vessels escaping upriver. Hasegawa remained silent when asked whether the attacking aircraft machine-gunned the survivors escaping in lifeboats.[30]

Even as late as December 21 the Japanese legation at The Hague officially sought to soften the gravity of the events which followed the initial bombing. The Japanese minister informed the American ambassador there that the motorboat attempted to approach the sinking vessel but had been attacked and for defensive reasons, returned the fire. Only when the attack had ceased, the minister had indicated, did the launch return and board the vessel. He told the American ambassador that the Japanese soldiers on the launch could not ascertain the nationality of the vessel at any time, although he neglected to mention the American flags that were flying and visibly painted on the superstructure.[31]

It now became increasingly clear to the State Department that the Japanese government was attempting to minimize the attack upon the gunboat after it became disabled as a result of the aerial bombardment and of the subsequent machine-gunning of the survivors. Non-committed members of the Roosevelt Administration now felt that unless the Japanese government met the demands of the United States in full, a grave diplomatic crisis would ensue between the two countries. Hull was also convinced at this point that the several Japanese investigations presently in progress would result in a stalemate as to which service group was most responsible for the disaster. In any case, the secretary felt that these investigations would conclude ultimately that the entire episode was solely the result of mistaken identity.

The first official Japanese naval investigation of the affair was completed by Captain Kondo on December 19; its findings were made known to Grew. According to Kondo, Japanese military units had received reports of Chinese troops crossing the Yangtze from Nanking to Pukow on the morning of December 12. Information also was received from units near Taiping that some ten steamers transporting Chinese troops were attempting to escape up the Yangtze. Only then were orders issued to Japanese military units to launch an attack upon these troops at Pukow. Kondo further indicated that at 9 a.m. on December 12, the adjutant of a Japanese battalion stationed in the near vicinity where the *Panay* and its convoy were anchored, halted the vessel and was informed by Hughes of the *Panay's* journey further upstream to withdraw out of range of hostilities. At 2:10 p.m. this same motor launch approached the area where the *Panay* had anchored to investigate the aerial attack upon the vessel. At this point, Kondo asserted that the commander of the motorboat assumed that the vessel was Chinese, since it was being bombarded by units of the Japanese naval air force and therefore the launch opened fire on the stricken gunboat. The Japanese naval commander failed to mention, however, any of the subsequent events which followed the initial attack.

It immediately appeared to Grew that either Kondo's findings were unclear as to whether the motorboat boarded the *Panay* after opening fire upon it, or he had ignored the matter entirely. Grew also noticed that the report failed to indicate whether the Japanese planes had machine-gunned the survivors in the lifeboats. Initially, Kondo admitted that only after the third bombing run did the pilots become aware of the mistaken identity. He later denied this, however, by claiming the pilots learned only on the following day that they had attacked and sunk an American gunboat.[32] Kondo's report emphasized the confusion which resulted from uncoordinated military operations between the army and navy during the siege of Nanking. The Japanese army command notified the navy of its belief that all neutral vessels still remained at Nanking on December 12. Hence, when the attack had been ordered, the pilots assumed that the *Panay* must have been Chinese. Kondo further impressed upon Grew that if the survivors were machine-gunned as subsequent evidence had shown, the pilots again assumed that they were Chinese abandoning their vessel.[33]

Grew forwarded Kondo's findings to Hull and while the secretary and State Department officials analyzed its contents, General Kumakichi Harada completed his investigation of the affair on December 20. The army's report varied widely from the accounts furnished by the vessel's survivors. According to the inquiry, the motor launch which approached the *Panay* on the morning of December 12 had warned the vessel to withdraw from the danger zone. When the initial bombing occurred Harada claimed that the *Panay* started to machine-gun Japanese troops along the river bank. He further denied that the launch callously attacked the sinking vessel. On the contrary, the launch, approaching the gunboat to rescue the survivors, was fired upon and in self-defense returned the fire. Even the army units which attempted to investigate the damages to the Standard Oil vessels, according to Harada, were attacked by the planes and several soldiers were killed or wounded.[34]

At a subsequent press conference held that afternoon, Harada admitted that he did not interview those individuals who had been directly involved in the episode but instead had relied heavily upon the testimony of his subordinate officers. He informed the press that he was unable to question those responsible due to the complexity of the Nanking operations and that the testimony from foreign eyewitnesses was strictly prohibited since "the questioning of foreign witnesses is not customary under Japanese military processes."[35]

Harada's findings appeared as an attempt to place the entire responsibility for the incident upon the Japanese Navy whose bombers were involved in the sinking. Grew, on the other hand, felt that both service units had issued orders to attack all vessels on the Yangtze even though each previously had known of the precise location of American ships in the vicinity. Indeed, the American ambassador remained skeptical that the worst still might occur over the incident. On December 20, following

Harada's report, he wrote in his diary that "if we can weather the storm . . . the net results of the incident will be to jolt the Japanese government that unless it exerts control over its army and navy, a breach of diplomatic relations is inevitable. . . ."[36]

The result of Harada's investigation was also forwarded to the State Department for consideration. Hull remained somewhat discontented over the Japanese investigations since they appeared to contradict each other in their findings. On December 22, he informed Grew that the Japanese pilots should have realized that they had attacked and destroyed an American vessel and had subsequently machine-gunned its survivors. The secretary could not understand how the Japanese investigations could have concluded otherwise or had failed to mention that the vessels were clearly distinguished by American flags in horizontal and vertical positions. Nor could Hull comprehend how the Japanese military authorities could have overlooked undisputed evidence showing that the *Panay's* location was dispatched to them almost hourly on December 12. Grew informed Hull of his proposed meeting with Japanese representatives who had conducted subsequent inquiries into the disaster and hoped that their findings would parallel the American version of the incident.[37]

On December 23, Grew met with several Japanese representatives in an effort to avert a possible stalemate between the two countries in their respective investigations. Commander Takada, a staff officer in the Japanese Navy, who had completed an on-the-spot investigation of the incident earlier, informed Grew of his findings. According to Takada, since December 11 naval air units had been receiving alarming reports of Chinese forces withdrawing from Nanking in vessels along the Yangtze. Takada claimed that at 4 p.m. on December 12 he had received a report by telephone as to the exact location of the *Panay* and its convoy of Standard Oil vessels. He could not believe, nor did the naval air force expect that the American convoy could have journeyed as far as 27 miles above Nanking. For this reason, the attack was ordered under the assumption that the gunboat formed a portion of Chinese vessels fleeing the area. Contrary to testimony from the previous and later Japanse findings, Takada asserted that both army and navy units were instructed not to attack foreign vessels but added that in the heat of battle, information concerning the presence of foreign vessels had been overlooked.

In contrast to the American account, Takada declared that minutes before the attack had actually occurred, fog made visibility difficult while the smoke from the guns on both sides also added to the failure in identifying the vessel's nationality. Japanese planes, he told Grew, attacked in groups of three and no plane attacked the same objective more than twice. When the bombing of the *Panay* began the Standard Oil vessels immediately anchored near shore and their crews started to abandon the tankers. From all appearances, according to Takada, the pilots believed that they were retreating Chinese soldiers, a fact which further enhanced the contention that the convoy was Chinese.

The Japanese naval investigator justified the attack on the lifeboats when he asserted that one of the planes fired its machine-guns while it was in the process of bombing the vessel. Moreover, army motor launches, according to naval information, could not have attacked the helpless gunboat and its crew since army units never advanced that far during the battle of Nanking. Even if army units had been in the vicinity, Takada believed that the Japanese commander would have assumed that the vessels under attack by their own planes would naturally have been Chinese.

Takada emphasized the point that the Japanese Navy attempted to aid the survivors after it was discovered that they had bombed an American convoy. A seaplane and two motor launches were sent to the area but they were attacked by Chinese troops and forced to withdraw. Admiral Isoroku Yamamoto, who was one of the originators of the Pearl Harbor attack four years later, supported Takada's testimony but added that since the motor boats had not been identified accurately, the navy stood ready to assume full responsibility for the sinking.[38]

Following Takada's report, Lieutenant Colonel Nishi, representing the Japanese Army, also conducted an investigation and informed the American ambassador of his findings. Nishi's probe into the affair was independent of Harada's inquiry, although he also attempted to minimize the army's responsibility. The army investigator told Grew that a small Japanese army unit had advanced with several motor launches to the approximate area where the incident occurred. The commander of the unit had observed the convoy at the time but could not identify its nationality and therefore dispersed his forces along the river bank in defensive positions. When the aerial bombardment on the *Panay* commenced, according to Nishi, the Japanese commander ordered two of his motor launches to attack any of the vessels which attempted to flee from the convoy. The unit commander assumed at this point that the convey consisted of Chinese vessels. When the *Meiping* and *Meihsia* anchored at Kaiyian wharf during the initial bombing run, the commander believed that the two vessels were attempting to escape and therefore opened fire with machine guns. No direct hits were made, however, due to the distance between the Japanese and American vessels.

Nishi concluded by pointing out that the army unit had learned of the identity of the convoy only when they ultimately boarded the anchored oil vessels. A motor boat was then dispatched by the Japanese commander to the sinking *Panay* in order to determine the condition of the gunboat. At that time, a second aerial attack occurred and the army unit on board the vessel vainly attempted to signal their identity to the attacking planes by waving Japanese flags. The bombardment, however, continued and two of the soldiers were killed and four were wounded.[39]

In the meantime, the American Court of Inquiry in Shanghai, composed of four members and headed by Captain H. V. McKittrick, concluded its investigation of the incident on December 23 and published its findings. The Court reiterated the purpose and mission of the *Panay* and confirmed the survivors' reports of the event leading to and including the actual attack.[40] The Japanese pilots, according to the Court's conclusions, should have been familiar with the characteristics and distinguishing marks of American vessels in general and the *Panay* in particular since the latter had been present at Nanking during their aerial attack on the city. Moreover, the Court could find no reason why the Japanese pilots attacked the convoy without first having identified the target, since it had been known that neutral vessels were in the Yangtze River throughout the campaign. Indeed, the Court further found it incomprehensible that none of the airplanes coming within 600 feet of the gunboat could identify the vessel's nationality even though sizeable American flags were flying and painted on the superstructure. Nor did the inquiry accept the Japanese version that the attack upon the sinking vessel by patrol boats and the subsequent machine-gunning of the lifeboats was a case of mistaken identity. The Court, therefore, ruled that the Japanese were entirely responsible for all losses which occurred as a result of the attack.[41]

Following the naval inquiry, Roosevelt informed his cabinet members that he believed the sinking was intentional. Up until then, the Japanese had insisted that the entire episode was a mistake on their part, but the President still remained unconvinced by the Japanese version. Roosevelt felt that freezing Japanese assets in the United States would bring them to terms without war and therefore he continued to explore these possibilities under the Trading With the Enemy Act in case Japan refused to accept fully the American naval court's findings. The cabinet members supported the President's contention while the secretary of navy reaffirmed his earlier statement that the fleet was in condition and could be placed in readiness in two weeks. Even military units, according to the secretary of the army, could be ordered to the West Coast if necessary at a moment's notice if some form of economic sanction were approved.[42]

As matters developed, there was no occasion for any retaliatory action on the part of the United States. On Christmas Eve, Hirota informed Grew that his government had accepted the American demands made in its note of December 14 but with some modifications. The Japanese government, he told the American ambassador, still believed that the incident was unintentional and due entirely to mistaken identity, not the result of an underlying disregard for American rights. The Japanese government agreed to the other provisions of the American demands such as full expressions of regret and compensation for all losses sustained in the sinking. The foreign minister then impressed upon Grew that the Japanese Navy had issued strict orders to "exercise the greatest caution in every area where warships and other vessels and nationals of America are present in order to avoid a recurrence of a similar mistake." Similar orders were also issued to the military forces throughout China; information concerning all non-belligerents was to be sent to the authorities on the spot. According to Hirota, those directly responsible for the attack had been removed from their posts and duly dealt with, although the foreign minister did not specify exactly what punishment had been prescribed. Hirota concluded by declaring:

> It is my fervent hope that the fact will be fully appreciated by the Government of the United States that this drastic step has been taken solely because of the sincere desire of the Japanese Government to safeguard the rights and interests of the United States and other third powers.[43]

Hirota's note was immediately forwarded to Hull who accepted its contents and informed Grew on Christmas Day that he was satisfied with the promptness by which the Japanese government "admitted responsibility, expressed regret and offered amends." The secretary made it clear, however, that the United States government would accept the conclusions reached by the American Naval Court of Inquiry and not the Japanese versions as to the causes and circumstances surrounding the incident. The American ambassador delivered Hull's note of December 25 to Hirota on the following day and the Japanese minister again assured Grew that his government would continue to employ measures to prevent future incidents from occurring.[44]

Though the Japanese note was accepted and a crisis averted, Roosevelt and several members of the Administration still remained skeptical of Japan's intentions to maintain the good will of the United States. The President felt that Japan did not give a completely satisfactory apology as he had requested. He did not know, for example, whether any punishment would be given by the Japanese government to those responsible for the sinking or whether Japan would pay the full amount for the losses sustained. Moreover, Japan considered the entire affair as an unintentional, unpremeditated error on the part of some of their overly-anxious military and naval units, an interpretation which was completely different from the American naval version. Roosevelt accepted the Japanese apology though he still remained convinced that the sinking was a deliberate attempt by the Japanese to rid China of American and the Western influence. In any event, he fully realized that an isolationist public would never accept any military action over an incident which had been settled, although Ickes, Morgenthau, and Swanson continued to believe that war between the two nations was inevitable and that the present was the most opportune moment for any chances of success.[45]

Frederick Moore, the State Department's Far Eastern expert, was also convinced that the attack had underlying motives. Moore blamed several jingoistic-minded military and naval officers, including Colonel Hashimoto, for the attack since they resented American interference with the Japanese campaign in China.[46] Even Yarnell remained pessimistic regarding future relations with Japan. In a letter to Grew, he declared that one of the essential long-range policies of Japan was the intention to force all foreigners from China. He predicted that the United States would become embroiled in future *Panay* incidents with Japan "unless the younger officers of the Japanese army change their tactics."[47]

While the United States government was assessing the damages sustained in the incident, cash donations from the Japanese people continued to arrive at the American Embassy in Tokyo. As of January 21, 1938, some $5,000 had been donated and in a note to Hull, Grew suggested that the money be accepted by the

Panay survivors, who, in turn, would subscribe the donations to deserving projects in Japan. Like Hull, Grew believed the money could be applied to worthy projects which would further enhance friendly relations between the two nations. Hull approved of Grew's proposal on February 12 and instructed him to formulate some arrangement along these lines. On February 28, Grew submitted a plan whereby the money would be held in perpetuity under a trust fund in Japan and that the United States ambassador, the Japanese president of the American Japan Society, and one other American nominated by the two members would be designated as the trustees of the fund. Both governments endorsed Grew's plan and the fund was later expanded and used to finance several projects in Japan.[48]

By March 21, the State Department completed the financial claims for indemnification and requested Grew to present the itemized account to the Japanese government. The account stipulated by the State Department was as follows:

A. PROPERTY LOSSES

1. Navy Department
   a. Loss of *Panay* — $ 455,727.87
   b. Loss of vessel's equipment, supplies, etc. — 97,766.48
   c. Effects of personnel — 40,263.00
       TOTAL — $ 593,757.35
2. Post Office Department
   a. Stamps, funds and supplies — 74.27
3. Department of State
   a. Effects of Embassy Personnel — 6,400.80
4. Standard Oil Company
   a. Loss of *Meiping, Meihsia* and *Meian* — 1,287,942.00
   b. Loss of personal property on board vessels — 57,495.59

    TOTAL of all property losses above mentioned — $1,945,670.01

B. DEATH AND PERSONAL INJURY INDEMNIFICATION

1. For death of two members of crew of *Panay* and Captain of *Meiping,* and injury to seventy-four people on board *Panay* and other vessels — 268,337.35

    GRAND TOTAL — $2,214,007.36[49]

The Japanese government, after consulting with several of their departments, accepted the itemized account and on April 30, Seijiro Yoshizawa, the Director of the Bureau of American Affairs of the Foreign Office, presented a check for $2,214,007.36 to Eugene H. Dooman, Counselor of the American Embassy in Tokyo.[50]

Five days before the Japanese payment was received, Swanson requested that another gunboat be constructed to replace the *Panay*. Roosevelt, however, did not favor the building of another Yangtze River vessel. Instead, the President indicated a preference for a different type of gunboat, such as a shallow draft vessel which he felt would be useful in the shallow waters among the islands in the Pacific or along the Mexican and South American coasts. Roosevelt refused to have the Japanese construct a vessel to replace the *Panay*. In any case, nothing further was done on the President's recommendation.[51]

Following the financial settlement of the *Panay* matter, the Japanese government asked the secretary of navy whether the Navy Department would approve of their salvaging the sunken vessel. Swanson informed the Japanese government that the transfer of the *Panay* to Japan would be a direct violation of Article 22 of the London Naval Treaty of 1936 which provided:

> No High Contracting Party shall by gift, sale, or any mode of transfer, dispose of any of His surface vessels of war or submarines in such a manner that such vessel may become a surface vessel or a submarine in any foreign navy.[52]

Swanson turned the matter over to the State Department for consideration. He told Hull, however, that correspondence and technical pamphlets on gunnery, etc., were still on board the *Panay* and therefore, he opposed the disclosure of what would be considered as national defense secrets. Moreover, a number of code and signal publications had been thrown overboard during the attack and these items would be found if salvage operations were carried out by the Japanese. Swanson added that certain Japanese items, including a bomb sight which had been taken from an airplane previously shot down, were still aboard the vessel. Hence, the secretary of navy urged Hull not to permit the Japanese to salvage the *Panay*. The secretary of state agreed with Swanson and on April 29 the Japanese request was denied by Hull.[53]

While the United States was in the process of resolving the *Panay* crisis, the British government also attempted to reach a settlement with Japan over the shelling of the *HMS Ladybird*. In a stern note to the Japanese government which parallaled the

American example, the British demanded full compensation, the prevention of further occurrences of this nature and general assurances for the safety of British nationals, ships, and other property. On December 14, Hirota tendered his government's profound apologies to the British ambassador in Tokyo for the attacks upon the vessels *Ladybird, Scarab,* and *Cricket* and informed Craigie that the shelling had been a mistake. The Japanese government, Hirota told the British representative, would take the necessary steps to compensate for the losses sustained and assured him that such incidents would not occur in the future. "It is the fervent hope of the Japanese Government," Hirota declared, "that the traditional friendship between Japan and Great Britain will not be affected by those unfortunate incidents."[54]

In a note dispatched to Hirota on the following day, the British foreign secretary pointed out that the Japanese apologies neglected to mention the attacks upon the merchant vessels such as the *Wangpu* and he therefore requested that specific assurances be given to all British vessels in the Far East. Eden also hoped that the Japanese army officers involved in the attacks would be removed and punished.

> Adequate punishment of those responsible for the particular attacks under discussion seems to his Majesty's Government the only method by which further outrages can be prevented. His Majesty's Government cannot but recall previous incidents in which the Japanese Government has expressed regret for attacks on British nationals and property and has given assurances that adequate steps had been taken to prevent any repetition.[55]

At this point, many members of Parliament who felt that British prestige had been weakened as a result of the attack, urged the Chamberlain government to dispatch more warships to Chinese waters. At the very least, they hoped the government would apply some type of economic sanctions against Japan as a future safeguard against such attacks. On December 22, Eden informed the House of Commons that since the United States had refused to reinforce its navy in the Far East, the British fleet would lack the necessary force, with or without reinforcements, to undertake unilateral naval action there. The foreign secretary also disapproved of initiating economic sanctions against Japan arguing that "no one should contemplate action of that kind in the Far East unless he is convinced that he had an overwhelming force to back that policy." Chamberlain reiterated a similar policy but assured anxious members of the House that the government would not remain indifferent to its international obligations or forgetful of its duty to protect British interests in China.[56]

Following a Japanese Army investigation into the *Ladybird* affair, Hirota indicated in a note to Craigie on December 28, that visibility had been made difficult when the vessels in question discharged black smoke in order to create a smoke screen. For this reason, Hirota maintained, the Japanese artillery commanders assumed that the vessels were Chinese and were attempting to escape from the Japanese shore batteries dispersed along the Yangtze. Craigie questioned the validity of the army version of the attack but nevertheless forwarded Hirota's note to London. Both Eden and Chamberlain were dissatisfied with the conclusions reached by the Japanese investigators and the failure to mention what, if any, disciplinary measures had been taken against the commanders involved. The British leaders, however, decided to close the *Ladybird* case if Japan offered an apology, assurances against future incidents and promised financial compensation.[57]

On December 30, the Japanese government accepted the British demands in full, though Hirota informed the British ambassador that the attack would still be considered the result of mistaken identity. The foreign minister reiterated his previous apologies and promised compensation; he stated that those responsible for the attack "had been dealt with according to military law." Concerning the British request for guarantees against future attacks, Hirota asserted that the Japanese naval and military authorities had received renewed instructions to take "the greatest possible care that attacks are not made upon the lives and property of British nationals." The Chamberlain government accepted the Japanese note, although they remained convinced that the artillery barrage upon the *Ladybird* had been intentional. Like Hull's reply ending the *Panay* crisis, the British Foreign Office informed the Japanese government that it would rely upon its own version of the attacks.[58]

Damage to the *Ladybird* and the other vessels involved was ultimately assessed at £2,942. This claim was presented to the Japanese government on August 18, 1938, and payment was made in full on August 31.[59]

Notes

[1] Cordell Hull, *Memoirs of Cordell Hull* (New York: The Macmillan Co., 1948), I, 559-560.

[2] U.S. Department of State, *Peace and War, United States Foreign Policy, 1931-1941* (Washington: GPO, 1943), pp. 519-520. Cited hereafter as *Peace and War, 1931-1941*.

[3] *New York Times*, December 14, 1937, p. 1.

[4] *Peace and War, 1931-1941*, p. 523; see also Elliott Roosevelt (ed.), *F.D.R. His Personal Letters, 1928-1945* (New York: Duell, Sloan and Pearce, 1950), II, 732-733. According to Hidenari Tarasaki, a prominent official in the Japanese Foreign Office, Roosevelt's note was never delivered to the Japanese Emperor. This fact did not become known to Roosevelt until early in December, 1941, when he again attempted to avert a war between the two nations by sending a note directly to the Emperor. Gwenn Terasaki, *Bridge to the Sun* (Chapel Hill: The University of North Carolina Press, 1957), p. 68.

[5] Conversation between Cordell Hull and Hiroshi Saito, December 13, 1937, Cordell Hull Papers, Manuscript Division, Library of Congress, Box 229. Cited hereafter as Hull Papers.

[6] *Peace and War, 1931-1941*, pp. 523-524.

[7] Grew to Hull, December 13, 1937. 394.115 Panay/30, National Archives, Record Group 59. Cited hereafter as NA, RG 59; see also *Peace and War, 1931-1941*, pp. 525-526.

[8] U.S. Department of State, *Foreign Relations of the United States, Diplomatic Papers, 1937* (Washington: GPO, 1954), III, 494-495. Cited hereafter as *Foreign Relations, 1937*.

[9] William D. Leahy, Diary, December 14, 1937, William D. Leahy Papers, Manuscript Division, Library of Congress. Cited hereafter as Leahy Papers.

[10] Johnson to Hull, December 13, 1937. 394.115 Panay/28 NA, RG 59; see also *Foreign Relations, 1937*, p. 491.

[11] *Foreign Relations, 1937*, pp. 798-800.

[12] *New York Herald Tribune*, December 14, 1937, p. 1.

[13] *New York Times*, December 15, 1937, p. 20.

[14] Roger Levy, *French Interests and Policies in the Far East* (New York: Institute of Pacific Relations, 1941), p. 67; *Foreign Relations, 1937*, p. 809; *Echo de Paris*, December 15, 1937, p. 4.

[15] *New York Times*, December 15, 1937, p. 16.

[16] Arnold Toynbee, *Survey of International Affairs* (London: Oxford University Press, 1938), I, 300; Phillips to Hull, December 15, 1937. 394.115 Panay/108 NA, RG 59.

[17] *New York Herald Tribune*, December 19, 1937, p. 2.

[18] U.S. Department of State, *Documents on German Foreign Policy, 1918-1945*, Series D (Washington: GPO, 1949), I, 654-656.

[19] *Peace and War, 1931-1941*, pp. 528-530.

[20] *Ibid.*, p. 526.

[21] *Foreign Relations, 1937*, p. 502.

[22] John M. Blum, *From the Morgenthau Diaries: Years of Crisis 1928-1938* (Boston: Houghton Mifflin Co., 1959), p. 486.

[23] *Ibid.*, p. 487.

[24] Harold L. Ickes, *The Secret Diary of Harold L. Ickes* (New York: Simon and Schuster Inc., 1959), II, 274-275.

[25] *Ibid.*

[26] Leahy Diary, December 16, 1937, Leahy Papers.

[27] *Peace and War 1931-1941*, p. 527.

[28] Conversation between Hull and Saito, December 17, 1937, Hull Papers; See also Hull to Grew, December 18, 1937. 394.115 Panay/160A. NA, RG 59.

[29] *Foreign Relation, 1937*, p. 509.

[30] Yarnell to the Navy Department, December 20, 1937. 394.115 Panay/232. NA, RG 59.

[31] The American Ambassador at The Hague to Hull, December 21, 1937. 394.115 Panay/171, NA, RG 59.

[32] *Peace and War, 1931-1941*, pp. 531-532.

[33] *Ibid.*, p. 532.

[34] *Foreign Relations, 1937*, p. 514.

[35] Shuhsi Hsu, *Japan and the Third Powers* (Shanghai: Kelly and Walsh Ltd., 1941), p. 149.

[36] Joseph Grew, *Ten Years in Japan* (New York: Simon and Schuster Inc., 1944), p. 236.

[37] *Foreign Relations, 1937*, p. 516.

[38] Conference between Grew and Japanese Representatives, December 23, 1937. 394.115 Panay/312. NA, RG 59.

[39] *Ibid.*

[40] For a detailed account of the Court's findings see *Foreign Relations, 1937*, pp. 196-200.

[41] *Ibid;* see also *Peace and War, 1931-1941*, p. 547.

[42] Ickes, pp. 276-277.

[43] *Peace and War, 1931-1941*, pp. 549-551.

[44] *Ibid.*, p. 552.

[45] Ickes, p. 279; see also Blum, p. 492.

[46] Frederick Moore, *With Japan's Leaders: An Intimate Record of Fourteen Years as Counsellor to the Japanese Government Ending December 7, 1941* (New York: Charles Scribner's Sons, 1942), p. 89.

[47] Yarnell to Grew, January 2, 1938, Harry E. Yarnell Papers, Manuscript Division, Library of Congress. Cited hereafter as Yarnell Papers.

[48] *Peace and War, 1931-1941*, pp. 555-559.

[49] *Ibid.*, pp. 561-563.

[50] *Chinese Weekly Review*, April 30, 1938, p. 242.

[51] Roosevelt to Swanson, April 25, 1938. OF 18, Franklin D. Roosevelt Papers, The Franklin D. Roosevelt Library, Hyde Park, N. Y.

[52] Swanson to Hull, April 28, 1938. PR 5/L11-1 Naval History Division, United States Department of Navy.

[53] *Ibid.*

[54] *The Manchester Guardian,* December 15, 1937, p. 16; see also *The Times* (London), December 15, 1937, p. 16.

[55] *New York Herald Tribune,* December 16, 1937, p. 1.

[56] *New York Herald Tribune,* December 22, 1937, p. 1; see also *The Manchester Guardian,* December 22, 1937, p. 4.

[57] *New York Times,* December 28, 1937, p. 1.

[58] *New York Herald Tribune,* December 28, 1937, p. 1.

[59] International Military Tribunal for the Far East, *Tokyo Trials: Proceedings of the Military Tribunal for the Far East* (Tokyo: Court House of the Tribunal War Ministry Bldg., 1946-1948), pp. 21, 371.

CHAPTER IV

THE LUDLOW REFERENDUM

Of the more immediate reactions to the sinking of the *Panay* and the subsequent crisis which it produced, none proved more significant than the referendum on war proposed by Louis Ludlow, a Democratic Congressman from Indiana. As one of the leading spokesmen for isolationism, Ludlow initiated the resolution in order to halt any possible attempts by the Administration to involve the nation in foreign conflicts. The proposed referendum also reflected the fears of most isolationists who believed that an aggressive President might lead the country into a war even though such a war might be opposed by the majority of the people. The Indiana congressman first proposed the referendum as early as February 14, 1935; it declared in essence:

> Except in the event of attack or invasion the authority of Congress to declare war shall not become effective until confirmed by a majority of all votes cast thereon in a Nationwide referendum.[1]

Ludlow defined his 1935 resolution more explicitly in a subsequent amendment on February 5, 1937, in which he asserted that a nationwide referendum would be conducted "except in the event of an actual invasion of the United States or its territorial possessions and attack upon its citizens residing therein." In other words, by the 1937 resolution, Ludlow sought to hamstring any administration from declaring war over isolated incidents overseas where a few American nationals might accidently become involved or even killed in a foreign conflict.[2]

Such amendments to the Constitution which Ludlow had proposed were not novel in American history. Following the First World War, several resolutions on war submitted in Congress proved to be more extreme than Ludlow's two proposals. In 1924, a bill was introduced in the House calling for a national referendum to determine whether the United States would declare war even if the nation had actually been invaded. The 1924 bill, however, was never brought out of committee hearing for a vote on the floor of the House.[3] A year later, another resolution was proposed whereby three-fourths of the members of both Houses would be required to vote for war. Like the preceding resolution, this bill also languished in the Judiciary Committee.[4] By 1928, twelve such amendments were proposed in Congress, although none was ever taken seriously. Not until the 1930's was there widespread interest shown in war referendums. In 1934, two such bills were introduced simultaneously in which Congress would be given the power to declare war only after the President had first submitted the declaration to the states. A special election would then be called by each governor for a vote on the declaration. The bills further stipulated that conscription would be permitted only if the draftee were not required to leave the North American continent. Both proposals were buried in committee and never brought up for passage.[5]

By early 1935, proponents for a war resolution received renewed impetus as a result of the Senate investigation headed by Gerald P. Nye of North Dakota which concluded that bankers and industrialists had been instrumental in stampeding Congress into the First World War. It was in the wake of this investigation that Ludlow submitted his first referendum which found wide support among congressmen, church and educational groups, peace societies, and labor organizations. A Gallup Poll taken at that time also revealed that 75 percent of those queried favored such a resolution.[6] Commenting on his proposal in a letter to Hatton W. Summers, chairman of the House Judiciary Committee, Ludlow reiterated the conclusions reached by Nye by indicating that profiteering had been the cause of America's entry into the First World War. He further maintained that his amendment would not only minimize the possibility of war but it would also remove the incentive to rush into a conflict. Summers and other members of the Judiciary Committee were not swayed by Ludlow's viewpoint and the resolution was tabled for further consideration. At this point, the Indiana Democrat filed a discharge petition to have the resolution brought out of committee. Under this procedure, 218 congressmen would be required to sign the petition before any action could be taken on the resolution. Though supported in many quarters, Ludlow secured only 74 signatures by the end of 1936, far below the 218 required.[7]

The isolationist congressman, nevertheless, renewed his efforts to obtain the requisite number of signatures and by December,

1936, informed Roosevelt in a letter that he would submit another more positive proposal during the next session of Congress. Basing the new resolution upon the sentiments of isolationists everywhere, he told the President "that those who have to fight and, if need be, to die and to bear the awful burdens and costs of war should have the right to say whether war should be declared." Ludlow informed Roosevelt that his projected proposal had already received the approval and support of 21 railroad brotherhoods, leaders of all Protestant denominations, the Women's Christian Temperance Union, the American War Mothers, and 65 university presidents.[8] Ludlow reiterated these views to his colleagues when the 75th Congress convened in January, 1937. He told members in a speech on January 14, that of the 435 Representatives and 96 Senators in Congress, war could be declared by no more than 218 Congressmen and 49 Senators or a total of 267 individuals; some 127 million Americans would have no voice over the matter. Such a small group, according to the Indiana Democrat, might be swayed to vote for war by the person who occupied the White House. Ludlow submitted his resolution officially the following month with the firm conviction that passage of his amendment would restrain any ambitious executive and would provide a greater voice for the citizen in decisions governing war.[9]

Ludlow immediately launched upon a vigorous program to secure the 218 necessary signatures while the National Council for Prevention of War and other pacifist groups organized an active campaign to pressure Congress to support the resolution. Such lobbying activity proved somewhat effective. A Gallup Poll taken in October, 1937, revealed that over 80 percent of those questioned believed that Congress should obtain the approval of the people before declaring war.[10]

On November 29, Ludlow issued an impassioned plea for his proposed 22nd amendment in a radio address to the nation. He told the radio audience that the government was autocratic when it determined the nation's foreign policy. "You can cast your ballot for a constable or a dogcatcher," he remarked, "but you have absolutely nothing to say about a declaration of war." Ludlow announced that such a resolution would keep the United States out of all foreign wars, though if the occasion ever arose, the country would wage a righteous war of defense. In countering arguments from opponents of the bill who believed that such a proposal would consume precious time in preparing the nation for war, Ludlow maintained that with modern means of transportation and communication a referendum could be held and completed in a matter of days.[11]

By the end of November, 1937, Ludlow had acquired 194 signatures favoring the resolution, although opponents still believed that the bill did not pose a serious threat to the established constitutional method of declaring war. A few of the bill's critics did prophesy that the referendum's growing popularity in the House might enable Ludlow to attain the required number of supporters. Avowed pacifist David J. Lewis, a Democratic Congressman from Maryland, had informed his colleagues of the referendum's potential strength, although he personally felt that such a resolution would be futile as a means in achieving permanent peace. "Instead of saving this country from a foreign war," he declared, "it is more likely to involve us in two wars, the foreign war and another war, here at home, civil in character, more to be dreaded than any other war."[12]

By the first week in December, Ludlow had 11 more signatures for his resolution for a total of 205 supporters; he still lacked 13 adherents. When Japanese naval planes had attacked and sunk the *Panay* on December 12, Ludlow believed that the anti-war sentiment in Congress would now be prevalent enough to obtain the remaining signatures for his resolution. His judgment not only proved accurate but in less than 24 hours following the sinking, Ludlow received the 13 additional signatures from previously hesitant congressmen who offered their full support to the referendum. Almost immediately the resolution posed as a serious challenge to the Administration's entire foreign policy, while critics were alarmed by the somewhat favorable public reaction it received. Though other so-called peace resolutions had been formulated in the past, the Ludlow amendment was the first ever to reach the floor of Congress; opponents of the bill fully realized that if passage proved successful, a severe domestic crisis might ensue. With the required 218 signatures now obtained, Ludlow discharged his petition from the House Judiciary Committee and House leaders scheduled a vote on January 10, 1938, as to whether the resolution should be brought out of committee and considered for debate on the floor of the House.[13]

With success now possible, the Ludlow forces accelerated their campaign to convince doubting lawmakers and the public in general that the executive should no longer be permitted to exercise dictatorial powers in the conduct of foreign affairs. The pacifist groups immediately pointed to the recent *Panay* crisis as a paramount example where the President could stampede the country into war with Japan if given unlimited freedom of action. Many supporters of the resolution, however, felt that it was a mistake to have forced the bill out of committee while Congress debated the *Panay* affair. They felt certain that the Administration would oppose the referendum and were not confident that the 218 members who had signed the petition would also vote for its ultimate passage. The more energetic supporters insisted that the resolution stood an excellent chance of succeeding; they argued that if the plan failed their cause would receive wide publicity for similar projects in the future.[14] To further promote the proposal, a National Committee for the War Referendum was established on December 22 under the direction of Major General William C. Rivers, retired. Rivers maintained that such a referendum would prevent any premature action from being taken by the Administration, particularly over the *Panay* episode. The retired army officer also felt that the referendum would not cause undue delay if a war situation were to occur.

> The people of this country undoubtedly are opposed to foreign war. A war referendum would not only give the people complete control over policies that lead to war but the effect of the people having the right to vote on war would make any administration more hesitant to follow a line of policy likely to result in a war situation.[15]

Though the immediate objectives of the organization were not achieved, their efforts did strengthen isolationist sentiment and embarrassed the Administration in its efforts to pursue a more positive policy against Japan over the *Panay* episode.[16]

While the War Referendum Committee was conducting its campaign, numerous radio addresses, press conferences and public pronouncements were given by government officials and leaders of other peace organizations favorable to the resolution. Among the more prominent senators supporting the Ludlow amendment was Gerald P. Nye who asserted that wars were instigated by a few individuals merely for economic profit. Nye felt certain that if the American people governed the decision of war and peace directly, then bankers, industrialists, or the executive branch would be unable to plunge the nation into a needless war. Senator Robert F. La Follette of Wisconsin reiterated a similar attitude when he told the press:

> A declaration of war can, without further check by the people, set up a virtual military dictatorship, send millions of men to death in foreign lands, open the gates to billions of war loans to foreign nations and burden down the nation with more than double the present national debt.[17]

Defending the referendum in a radio address, Democratic Congressman H. P. Koppelmann of Connecticut, maintained that the Ludlow amendment would effectively check any demands for war over future sinkings comparable to the *Panay*. In another radio broadcast, Democratic Congressman Herbert S. Bigelow of Ohio, sought a stronger isolationist policy in foreign affairs by advocating enactments prohibiting conscription of Americans to fight on foreign soil.

> When a Government by act of a President and the votes of 267 men in Congress, puts you on transports and ships you to foreign lands, to fight and die on foreign soil and shoots you if you protest, there is just one name to give to that—it is mass slavery.[18]

Bigelow's colleague in the House, Hamilton Fish, Jr. of New York, did not favor such drastic measures as ending conscription, though he supported the Ludlow Referendum avidly. As the leading minority member of the Committee on Foreign Affairs, Fish was opposed to American intervention in foreign entanglements and believed the people should determine this issue instead of the government.[19]

Outside of Congress, various peace groups and pacifist organizations campaigned actively for the referendum and many of the labor associations voiced their approval of the amendment. Several labor groups which went on record in favor of the resolution were the Railway Labor Executives Association, the Brotherhood of Painters, Decorators and Paperhangers, the Minnesota Federation of Labor, and the American Federation of Teachers. Among the churches, the Evangelical Lutheran Augustana Synod of North America informed Hatton W. Summers in a letter that they had voted unanimously at their annual convention in December to support the Ludlow Referendum. Other church groups also sent petitions to Congress urging the adoption of the proposal.[20]

Florence B. Boeckel, Secretary of the National Council for Prevention of War, summed up the views of her organization in a press conference on January 2, 1938. According to Mrs. Boeckel, Ludlow's constitutional amendment would be one more bulwark against involvement in foreign wars, although it would not interfere with the nation's defense. The peace societies, she told the press, believed that the President was following a definite and aggressive line of foreign policy which could embroil the nation in a crisis and leave Congress no alternative but to declare war.[21] Other peace societies such as the Women's International League for Peace and Freedom, the Fellowship of Reconciliation, and the Emergency Peace Campaign all adopted a similar outlook, and Mrs. Estelle Sternberger, Executive Secretary of World Peaceways, informed the press:

> The people of the United States will not be satisfied with the formality of having the Ludlow resolution reported out of committee. The recent developments in China have made the people realize that a nation can be certain of keeping out of war only if the people hold the power over declarations of war.

Joseph H. Fussel, Secretary-General of the Theosophical Society, offered a similar opinion to the press and further added that the amendment would not only offer a safeguard to the American people against war but would serve as an example for other nations to follow.[22]

Oswald G. Villard was one of the most prominent journalists who supported the Ludlow Referendum. Writing for *The Nation* magazine, Villard maintained that the proposed amendment would not inhibit American foreign policy in any particular crisis if the President disregarded war as a means to an end. Although history was to prove him wrong four years later, Villard believed that if the Japanese destroyed the American Pacific fleet "we should have plenty of time to mobilize and to await the taking of the referendum on whether the American people wish to plunge the country into war to avenge the loss of those ships."[23]

While the Ludlow Referendum was debated and analyzed both in and out of Congress, other so-called peace amendments were submitted simultaneously in the Senate. These bills were sponsored by Senators Nye, La Follette, Bennett C. Clark, and Arthur Capper, who hoped that one of their proposals would be adopted in the Senate as a substitute referendum in the event the Ludlow bill passed the House but failed in the upper chamber. In principle, each of the Senate resolutions was similar to the Ludlow amendment. The Nye resolution, for example, asserted that if an actual invasion of the United States occurred Congress would then be empowered to declare war, while the Clark and La Follette resolutions added that Congress could declare war if American territories were invaded or if any other North American or Caribbean nation were subjected to attack. Senator Capper clarified his resolution more specifically than his colleagues when he asserted that Congress could declare war "when the President proclaims that territory subject to its jurisdiction has been invaded or is in immediate danger of invasion." Capper first announced his resolution as early as November 30, 1937, in a radio address to the nation in which he outlined a six-point program that he considered mandatory in preserving American isolationism:

1. Keep out of the League of Nations and steer clear of alliances.
2. Keep American warships in home waters and withdraw American citizens from war zones.
3. Keep American soldiers at home.
4. Keep American dollars at home when invited to invest them to finance other nations' wars.
5. Invoke the provisions of the Neutrality Act.
6. The passage by Congress of his or any other war referendum already submitted.[24]

The four proposals were referred to the Senate Judiciary Committee but languished there following the result of the vote on the Ludlow amendment in the House.

While proponents of the referendum were campaigning actively for its passage, opposing groups challenged the imperative need for such a change in the Constitution. Critics of the proposal believed that this display of appeasement had greatly weakened the American diplomatic stand over the *Panay* episode at a crucial time and they were convinced that any referendum of this nature would endanger American interests and nationals in future conflicts. Since force is the final measurement of power, the amendment, according to critics, would leave the United States impotent against foreign encroachments. The opposition further maintained that many isolationists, despite their humanitarian sentiments toward the oppressed, nevertheless would dare not run the risk of war in order to check aggression in the world. Such a referendum would be unacceptable to internationalist-minded groups who felt that the United States should not only protect its world-wide commercial and shipping interests, by war if necessary, but also oppose injustice in the world. The anti-isolationists pointed out that wars, even the most futile or inequitable, were seldom declared without general approval at the time. Opponents of the bill also added that the amendment would abort the fundamental principles of the Monroe Doctrine by informing the world of America's unwillingness to resist attacks on Central and South America. Such a proposal, they argued, would further place American armed forces at a great disadvantage by the delay in conducting the plebiscite while the amendment would be equivalent to depriving the government of diplomatic procedures against treaty-breaking powers.[25]

Newspaper reaction, in particular, was unusually severe in its criticism of the Ludlow Referendum. Typical of this editorial expression was the *New York Times* which maintained that the entire United States fleet could be sunk anywhere overseas but under the amendment, the government could not retaliate until a nationwide referendum was held. "The Ludlow resolution," a later editorial declared, "would be taken as a notice to the world at large that the American people would not fight until long after the outer defenses of its diplomacy had been broken through and that venturesome Powers could safely disregard the warnings of our Presidents."[26] The *New York Herald Tribune,* in commenting on the Ludlow amendment, remarked that despite the undeniable logic of the referendum, "it is no less a lunatic proposal." The *Herald Tribune* viewed the appearance of the petition simply as a gesture which indicated the anti-war feeling in the country following the *Panay* sinking but felt it was hardly pretentious enough to warrant its importance. If the amendment were adopted, according to the newspaper editorial, any administration determined to plunge the nation in a conflict would be able to prepare for the referendum by playing upon public emotion for war.

> To restrict the power of Congress would not prevent the Secretary of State or the President from involving the country in quarrels with foreign countries or from appealing directly to the people for support. The President, in spite of the amendment, would still be commander-in-chief of the army and navy and have direction of foreign policy.[27]

In an editorial, the *Washington Post* censured the referendum and asserted that its passage would lead Japanese militarists "to assume that in the face of intense pacifist sentiment in Congress, the President would be hamstrung in his efforts to protect our legitimate interests in the Far East." The newspaper added caustically that if the Ludlow resolution had been passed before the *Panay* episode had occurred, the gunboat would have been required to hold its fire until a national referendum had taken place. The *Chicago Daily News* opposed the referendum fervently and viewed it "as an idea that could be harbored only by persons utterly ignorant of the realities of international life and death." The newspaper editorial pointed out that passage of the amendment would simply make the world safer for aggression and would serve notice that all nations could ignore the rights of American citizens abroad. A *San Francisco Chronicle* editorial expressed a similar attitude and maintained that such a referendum would enable aggressor nations to "assail our rights all they liked provided they did not actually invade our territory."[28]

The isolationist *Portland Oregonian* upbraided the referendum as inexpedient and questioned the proposal's validity. The passage of such an amendment, according to the newspaper, would create less respect for the United States in international affairs. The *Boston Globe* also refuted the resolution, maintaining that the referendum would merely create "immobilizing delays, lengthy debates, and filibusters in 48 legislatures and bitter emotional division of the country." To the *Globe,* the referendum would cripple American powers of self-defense and would impair the success of American diplomacy in the future. The *Dallas Morning News* branded the Ludlow Referendum as more idealistic than practical and blamed isolationists for pursuing a policy "that has helped stir world turmoil by keeping the United States aloof from world efforts to assure peace." The *Philadelphia Inquirer* took a more moderate attitude in praising the ideals of the referendum but nevertheless, believed that the proposal would disclose to other nations "a serious division of American opinion that might prove to be a direct incitement to quick hostile action against us." In an editorial, the *St. Louis Post-Dispatch* commended the well-meaning intentions of those responsible in submitting the referendum but claimed that the plan was neither wise nor pragmatical. The editorial pointed out that the referendum could result in an affirmative vote for war at a time when Congress did not wish to declare war. Moreover, a close vote for war might divide the nation in pursuing the war effort at a critical time.[29]

The *Cincinnati Inquirer* joined the majority of newspapers in condemning the referendum as being "foolhardy and unsound." The *Inquirer* criticized the resolution particularly for attempting to "sabotage the skillful and soundly conceived Far Eastern policy which the State Department is seeking to carry out." The newspaper added that under such a proposed law, American armed forces would be employed only when the outer defenses of the United States were penetrated by a prospective invader. According to a *Seattle Daily Times* editorial, the United States would not enter into an unnecessary war even if a war referendum had not been proposed. "If this country were threatened," the *Daily Times* editorial retorted, "any President will move the army and navy into action and any Congress will back him up and so will the nation." The *Detroit Free Press* viewed the referendum as "absurd and vicious" and contended that Congress was not complimenting the intelligence and maturity of the American people when it seriously considered the proposed amendment. The *Rocky Mountain News,* in commenting on the referendum, declared that such a proposal "would be an open invitation to pro-war propaganda and patriotic terrorism and would make a mockery of the democratic process." The isolationist-oriented *Minneapolis Tribune* vilified the referendum and warned that the resolution would bind Congress rigidly in an emergency. The *Tribune* editors believed that such a plan might easily develop a minor crisis into a major incident and eventual war. The *Christian Science Monitor* also viewed the Ludlow referendum as an illusory proposition which would not keep the United States permanently aloof from international problems.[30]

A *Milwaukee Journal* editorial expressed its opposition to the referendum "because we think that it would not safeguard the nation but would only complicate the handling of our foreign policy." The *Journal* objected to the grave inconsistencies encompassing Ludlow's resolution. If Brazil were invaded, for example, the United States could intervene actively if for no other reason than to uphold the Monroe Doctrine, but if an American national were killed in China or elsewhere Congress would be powerless to act under the amendment which Ludlow proposed. The *New Orleans Times-Picayune* indicated in an editorial that the American people would never permit pacifist groups to undermine the government's foreign policy by means of a war referendum. "Our national need is not a sentimental strait-jacket," the newspaper contended, "but a free hand with ample preparedness to take care of our institutions." The *Atlanta Journal* voiced a similar attitude and added that the Ludlow amendment would paralyze American foreign policy, enhance aggression, and deprive American forces of military superiority.[31]

The *Buffalo Evening News* frankly discussed and analyzed the advantages and disadvantages of the proposed amendment and asserted that what the government needed was not a modification in the method of declaring war, but that "neutrality must be made a principle, not a matter of expediency." The *Providence Journal* also pointed out the shortcomings of the referendum and argued that Ludlow had apparently failed to take into full account the speed and mobility of modern fighting forces as well as the damaging effects such a proposal would have upon foreign trade. "Notwithstanding these deficiencies," the newspaper added, "Ludlow's bill would merely serve as a prestige-losing measure in which nations such as Japan would consider it a sign of weakness." The *Butte Standard* (Montana) reiterated the same viewpoint when it maintained that if Ludlow's proposal were approved, Japan and other aggressive nations would seize upon the opportunity to defy American interests and demands. The *Los Angeles Times* felt that the referendum would not only handicap the executive in dealing with crucial diplomatic problems but would also weaken the prestige of the office to command any respect from other nations. The *Sacramento Union* implored Congress not to permit itself to be persuaded into favoring the resolution while a *Newark Evening News* editorial asserted that such a constitutional amendment would:

> Distort the balance of our scheme of government, tie the hands of the Executive, expose our national defenses to grave dangers at moments of international crisis and subject the vital issues of war and peace to political pulling and hauling.[32]

Other newspapers which voiced similar expressions of disapproval for the referendum included the *Birmingham News,* the *Salt Lake City Tribune,* the *Baltimore Sun,* and the *Louisville Times,* while a *Cleveland Plain Dealer* editorial remarked that "America is territorially too large to be run politically like a town meeting." In Ludlow's home state, an *Indianapolis Star* editorial praised the Indiana Democrat for pursuing the resolution. The editorial was doubtful, however, that the proposal would be adopted by Congress. "He may not attain his goal of a constitutional amendment," the editorial indicated, "but many a Congressman would not have gone as far as he has." The *Christian Century* summarized what little magazine reaction occurred over the Ludlow Referendum by commenting that such a proposal "would weaken rather than extend the authority of democracy in this country." The magazine maintained that the amendment would merely subject American foreign affairs to a greater degree of propaganda and that it would split the nation hopelessly in times of crisis.[33]

In editorials, several British newspapers and periodicals opposed the Ludlow amendment and urged the American Congress to defeat the measure. The *Manchester Guardian* believed that the plan would place a serious handicap on American statesmen in dealing with foreign powers. "To a certain extent," the newspaper asserted, "all democratic Governments must suffer from an inability to pledge their people in advance and to increase this handicap might prove fatal." The *Economist* (London) viewed the amendment with dismay and hoped that American foreign policy would be "left out of the arena of party hostility." The *Times* (London) and the *London Observor* also expressed a similar opinion while the *London Survey of International Affairs* of 1938, in commenting on the resolution, predicted optimistically that the American people would ultimately abandon isolationist policies

such as the plan Ludlow proposed. "With every new act of violence," the *Survey* proclaimed, "the American people will be
roused into giving expression to their strong condemnation of
Fascist methods."[34]

In the fascist nations, newspapers in Germany as well as the
Nazi government refrained from commenting on the Ludlow Referendum while the Japanese press and the government also ignored
the debate over the proposed amendment. In Italy, on the other
hand, Mussolini remarked candidly in the government's official
organ, *Popolo d' Italia,* that "Congresman Ludlow has had the
unpardonable candor of taking democracy seriously." The Duce
believed that American citizens should be allowed to express their
views on peace and war and also to determine the foreign policy
of the United States. Those democrats who opposed the resolution, he argued, merely proved that they feared the consequences
of their doctrines.[35]

While many isolationists and pacifist groups professed their
support for the referendum, a number of organizations crusaded
assiduously for its defeat. The Committee for Concerted Peace
Efforts endorsed Roosevelt's theory of quarantining aggressors and
asserted that "the menace to our peace and prosperity cannot be
avoided by a policy of isolation and neutrality." The committee
maintained that war could be eluded only if the inviolability of
treaties were sustained. They urged the government to lead the
way to world leadership.[36]

Military groups and individuals who opposed the referendum
felt that the measure would be detrimental to the national safety.
General John A. Lejeune, ex-commander of the Marine Corps,
believed that its adoption would deprive the nation of the opportunity to strike the first blow against an invader. Daniel J.
Doherty, national commander of the American Legion, announced
in a statement of policy on January 8, 1938, that the referendum
would not only seriously impair the functions of the State Department but would intimate a lack of confidence on the part of the
American people in their government. Doherty believed that the
entire strategy of national defense would be disrupted and that
other nations would interpret the amendment as a sign of weakness.
Supporting this attitude was Millard W. Rice, legislative representative of the Veterans of Foreign Wars, who declared that the
Ludlow amendment would:

1. Invite aggressor nations to flagrantly violate the rights of the
   United States.
2. Discourage friendly and orderly intercourse among nations.

3. Subject the people to conflicting intensive propaganda campaigns which would inflame a majority vote for war and arouse the resistance of the minority.
4. Destroy the representative form of government.
5. Weaken the defense of the nation.
6. Encourage undeclared warfare.[37]

Like other veteran associations in the country, the Yankee Division of New York implored Congress to defeat the measure since "it would be destructive of our national morale and disastrous in its efforts on our national defenses." As the leading literary spokesman for the military organizations, the *Army and Navy Journal* remarked that:

> Mr. Ludlow seems to forget that America has embarked upon war only when such a state is existing and that congressional finding merely confirms the fact of battle. To hold a referendum under such conditions would be to offer encouragement to the enemy.[38]

Opposition to the Ludlow Referendum also came from diversified elements throughout the country. The Southeastern Governors Conference, for example, announced in a resolution at its annual meeting held in early January, that they would support those groups who were against the referendum. Among the church leaders who opposed the amendment, Methodist Bishop William T. Manning declared in a statement to the press:

> Such action as that proposed might paralyze the defensive power of our nation. This is one of those unwise and ill-considered measures which in the name of peace would play into the hands of those who wish to make war.[39]

Other prominent figures likewise indicated their disapproval for the Ludlow amendment to the press. Radio commentator Elmer Davis, in a letter to the *New York Times,* maintained that the referendum would injure national unity by advertising to the world the differences of opinion which might exist in a crisis. He believed that such a resolution would be dangerous since "the whole American navy might be sunk in foreign waters and it would still be impossible for the government to mobilize the nation for self-defense until a vote has been taken."[40] Former Secretary of State Henry L. Stimson, in another letter to the *New York Times,* offered his support to the Amendment's opponents and asserted that the proposal would destroy the present system of national defense and make any defensive system ineffective if not impossible. Stimson warned that the acceptance of such a referendum system would not only weaken the American armed forces but would also impair national solidarity and would "invite other nations to regard us as showing instability in policy and behavior."[41]

In Congress, those members who had refuted the Ludlow amendment from its inception now embarked upon a campaign to convince hesitant congressmen of the measure's fallacies. In the Senate, Arthur H. Vandenberg of Michigan viewed the proposed referendum as "highly dangerous rather than protective" while Willliam H. King of Utah indicated his amazement that the proposal mustered such support. "This is equivalent to telling a nation like Japan," King asserted, "to go ahead and slap us in the face! Anything you do is all right with us." Clyde L. Herring of Iowa was more caustic toward the amendment when he told the press:

> This proposal presupposes that the elected representatives of the people are not sound, well-balanced legislators. If the people haven't faith in us, they should remove us from office. It would be a calamity to hamstring Congress. Why elect representatives and make them powerless on important issues?[42]

In the House, Democratic Congressman Robert L. Ramsey of West Virginia was convinced that the referendum would create a loss of prestige abroad, while Emmanuel Celler of New York maintained that any foreign power could invade Alaska and Hawaii before any declaration of war was passed. Celler's colleague, John J. O'Connor, also from New York, reiterated this viewpoint when he indicated that the proposal would involve the nation in war instead of preventing it. Under such a measure, according to O'Connor, a substantial increase in the country's armed forces and its fortifications would be necessary.[43]

Democratic Congressman Charles I. Faddis of Pennsylvania viewed the referendum primarily from an economic standpoint. Faddis felt certain that the resolution would not stop profiteering by a few individuals during wartime as Ludlow had professed inasmuch as "the commerce of the nation is in reality the commerce of all the people in the nation." The Pennsylvania Democrat pointed out that the United States still depended upon other countries for many essential products. Any interruption in this normal flow of trade, he claimed, would create a national catastrophe. "Those in charge of our national defense," he predicted, "must be left free to act quickly in time of emergency or dire consequences may very easily result." S. D. McReynolds, a Democrat from Tennessee and chairman of the House Foreign Relations Committee, criticized the Ludlow resolution in a radio address to the nation on December 28, 1937. He told the radio audience that the measure "would be absolutely misunderstood by those who

wish to misunderstand American policy and mislead their people."
McReynolds believed that the Ludlow amendment, coupled with
the recent *Panay* incident, would begin a chain reaction demanding
the withdrawal of American interests everywhere. A retreat of this
kind by a powerful nation, he cautioned, would influence other
less powerful states to retreat at the demands of aggressor
powers. Such an occurrence would cause treaty violations and
ultimate war.[44]

The Roosevelt Administration strongly opposed the referendum
and actively attempted to pressure recalcitrant House members
who had signed the discharge petition to vote against the measure
on January 10, 1938. Roosevelt did not reveal his own views on
the matter until December 17, when he denounced the referendum
in a press conference as "incompatible to the security of the
nation."[45] Hull also objected to the amendment and informed
McReynolds in a letter that "this plan would most seriously handicap the Government in the conduct of our foreign affairs generally
and would thus impair disasterously its ability to safeguard the
peace of the American people."[46] The Administration's opinion
on the Ludlow proposal was supported by GOP leader Alfred M.
Landon, the 1936 Republican presidential candidate. Landon
congratulated Roosevelt in a telegram on December 20 for the
unalterable stand which the President had taken in opposing the
referendum. "Many members of Congress from both parties," the
Republican leader wrote, "seem to have forgotten the basic principle of American politics and wish to create the impression on
foreign nations that they do not trust your administration of foreign
affairs." In offering his support to Roosevelt, Landon strengthened
the Administration's position on the measure and revealed ostensibly that Republican leaders opposed the isolationist movement in
general and the Ludlow resolution in particular.[47]

During the first week in January, 1938, the Administration
continued to exert its influence to have the measure defeated.
Louis Johnson, the Assistant Secretary of War, echoed the sentiments of the bill's opponents when he told members of the
University Club in Los Angeles on January 5 that passage of the
resolution would reduce the President to a mere figurehead in
diplomatic affairs and it would divest the State Department of its
importance. Johnson explained that it would be entirely possible
for an unfriendly European or Asiatic power to organize or support
a revolutionary army in Lower California or at any other point
and could endanger the security of the United States. He indicated
that under the provisions of the Ludlow amendment the govern-

ment would be powerless to counter such a threat. Johnson then pointed out other general weaknesses of the proposed referendum:

1. It is incompatible with a large industrialized nation.
2. The average citizen has neither the training nor the experience to decide the complex matter involved.
3. It is the antithesis of representative government.
4. The time element involved in the voting process would defeat any military advantage.
5. It would virtually prohibit the President from using diplomacy to prevent war such as in the *Panay* incident.[48]

On January 6, Roosevelt further indicated his disapproval of the Ludlow measure in a letter to Speaker of the House William B. Bankhead. The President informed the House Speaker that the referendum was "impracticable in its application and incompatible with our representative form of government." Roosevelt impressed upon Bankhead the damaging effect such an amendment would have upon any President who attempted to direct the foreign affairs of the nation. "I fully realize," he wrote, "that the sponsors of this proposal sincerely believe that it would be helpful in keeping the United States out of war but I am convinced it would have the opposite effect."[49]

When debate on the Ludlow proposal occurred on January 10, 1938, opponents of the bill issued fervent pleas for its defeat. Bankhead left the speaker's chair and read the letter which he had received from the President to House members while floor leader Sam Rayburn informed his colleagues that the referendum "would do more to plunge this nation into war than any action Congress could take." It was Roosevelt's opposition coupled with political pressure to end patronage to Democrats who supported the measure which convinced 55 congressmen to reverse their stand and help defeat the measure 188-209. In the final vote, 111 Democrats, 64 Republicans and 13 Progressives and Farm-Laborites supported the resolution while 188 Democrats and 21 Republicans opposed it. Geographically, congressmen from the farming districts in the Midwestern and Plain states supported the measure by a vote of better than two to one. Approximately three-fourths of the 209 members who voted against the proposal came from New York, Pennsylvania, Illinois and the Southern states. Congressmen from the rest of the nation were split almost evenly.[50]

In editorials most newspapers throughout the country praised the defeat of the referendum, although several indicated their discontent that the measure had not been defeated more severely. The *San Francisco Chronicle* summarized this skepticism accurately when it remarked in an editorial that "it is incredible that 43 per cent of the House membership could be so misguided as to follow their emotions and not their logic, to impose a national referendum upon any declaration of war." In Ludlow's home territory, the *Indianapolis Star* did not comment either way on the referendum's defeat in the House. The *Des Moines Register,* however, believed that through the resolution's defeat "some good has been accomplished if only in showing how deep the anti-war sentiment is in Congress." As one of the few newspapers which supported the amendment from the start, the *Register* was convinced that the close vote in the House would exercise an effective check on Roosevelt's foreign policy in the future. Indeed, most supporters of the resolution believed that the close vote in Congress offered a prime indication of the growing movement toward a stronger isolationist program; they prophesied that a foreign policy based on appeasement would soon be favored by the nation. Critics, on the other hand, viewed the failure of the amendment as the high watermark of pacifist sentiment and considered its defeat as a realistic approach 'to international problems. Proponents of internationalism pointed to the successful handling of the *Panay* affair which, they felt, proved that the executive could manage effectively a potential conflict with national dignity and at the same time remove the dangers of war.[51]

Roosevelt fully recognized that the Ludlow amendment represented one of the major obstacles by which isolationists had attempted to undermine his control of American diplomacy. Such an alternative, he felt, would have been disastrous to the nation. Roosevelt reiterated this feeling in a letter to his son, James, on January 20, 1938, when he wrote:

> National defense represents too serious a danger, especially in these modern times where distance has been annihilated, to permit delay and our danger lies in things like the Ludlow Amendment which appeal to people, who frankly have no conception of what modern war, with or without a declaration of war, involves.[52]

Roosevelt was well aware that isolationists still wielded an influence in shaping the course of American foreign policy. But he also realized that world events were menacing the security and vital interests of the United States. The recent crisis with Japan over the *Panay* sinking, in addition to the unexpected support and praise which he had received belatedly for his quarantine speech during the course of the debate on the Ludlow issue, helped convince Roosevelt to pursue a more positive military program, particularly in the area of naval expansion.

Notes

[1] House Joint Resolution 167, 74th Cong., 1st Sess., Papers Accompanying Specific Bills and Resolutions. National Archives, Legislative Division. Cited hereafter as NA, LD.

[2] House Joint Resolution 199, 75th Cong., 2nd Sess., NA, LD.

[3] House Joint Resolution 134, 69th Cong., 1st Sess., NA, LD.

[4] House Joint Resolution 40, 69th Cong., 2nd Sess., NA, LD.

[5] House Joint Resolutions 218 and 313, 73rd Cong., 2nd Sess., NA, LD.

[6] U.S., Department of State. *Public Attitude Studies* (Washington: GPO, 1941), p. 32.

[7] Letter from Ludlow to Summers, April 3, 1935. NA, LD; Dorothy Borg, *The United States and the Far Eastern Crisis of 1933-1938* (Cambridge: Harvard University Press, 1964), p. 503.

[8] Letter from Ludlow to Roosevelt, December 21, 1936, OF 274, Franklin D. Roosevelt Papers, The Franklin D. Roosevelt Library, Hyde Park, New York. Cited hereafter as Roosevelt Papers.

[9] U.S., Congress, House, *Ludlow Referendum on Participation in Foreign Wars,* 75th Cong., 2nd Sess., 1937, pp. 45-46.

[10] George Gallup and Saul F. Rae, *The Pulse of Democracy* (New York: Simon and Schuster Inc., 1940), p. 315.

[11] Radio Address by Louis Ludlow, November 29, 1937. NA, LD.

[12] *Congressional Digest,* 17 (February, 1938), 57.

[13] Robert A. Divine, *The Reluctant Belligerent: American Entry Into World War II* (New York: John Wiley and Sons, Inc., 1965), p. 48.

[14] *Congressional Digest,* 17 (February, 1938), 37.

[15] Ludlow Referendum, OF 3084, Roosevelt Papers.

[16] Attitudes of Organized Pressure Groups, 1920-1941, p. 20. Transcript summary in the Historical Division, United States Department of State.

[17] Wayne S. Cole, *Senator Gerald P. Nye and American Foreign Relations* (Minneapolis: The University of Minnesota Press, 1962), p. 121; *Foreign Policy Bulletin,* 17 (December 24, 1937), 3.

[18] U.S., *Congressional Record,* 75th Cong., 3rd Sess., 1938, LXXXIII, Part 9, Appendix, 25, 533.

[19] *Ibid.,* p. 234.

[20] Public Attitudes on the Ludlow Referendum, December 1937-January 1938, Transcript summary in NA, LD.

[21] *Congressional Digest,* 17 (February, 1938), 49.

[22] *Literary Digest,* 125 (January 1, 1938), 7.

[23] *Congressional Digest,* 17 (February, 1938), 50-51.

[24] *Ibid.,* 41-44.

[25] *New Republic,* 93 (December 29, 1937), 212-213; *Foreign Policy Bulletin,* 17 (December 24, 1937), 3.

[26] *New York Times,* December 16, 1937, p. 26; December 22, 1937, p. 24.

[27] *New York Herald Tribune,* December 16, 1937, p. 28; January 10, 1938, p. 2.

[28] *Washington Post,* December 16, 1937, p. 9; *Chicago Daily News,* December 18, 1937, p. 14; *San Francisco Chronicle,* December 17, 1937, p. 16.

[29] *Portland Oregonian,* December 17, 1937, P. 10; *Boston Globe,* January 11, 1938, p. 14; *Dallas Morning News,* January 11, 1938, p. 2; *Philadelphia Inquirer,* December 17, 1937, p. 14; *St. Louis Post-Dispatch,* December 17, 1937, p. 2.

[30] *Cincinnati Inquirer,* December 17, 1937, p. 4; *Seattle Daily Times,* December 18, 1937, p. 6; *Detroit Free Press,* December 18, 1937, p. 6; *Rocky Mountain News,* December 18, 1937, p. 4; *Minneapolis Tribune,* December 18, 1937, p. 18; *Christian Science Monitor,* December 16, 1937, p. 20.

[31] *Milwaukee Journal,* January 10, 1938, p. 10; *New Orleans Times-Picayune,* December 16, 1937, p. 10; *Christian Century* 55 (January 5, 1938), p. 8.

[32] *Buffalo Evening News,* December 20, 1937, p. 22; *Providence Journal,* December 18, 1937, p. 10; *Butte Standard* (Montana), December 27, 1937, p. 4; *Los Angeles Times,* December 23, 1937, p. 4; *Sacramento Union,* December 19, 1937, p. 6; *Newark Evening News,* January 11, 1938, p. 8.

[33] *Birmingham News,* January 11, 1938, p. 6; *Salt Lake City Tribune,* January 12, 1938, p. 10; *Baltimore Sun,* January 11, 1938, p. 8; *Louisville Times,* January 11, 1938, p. 8; *Cleveland Plain Dealer,* January 11, 1938, p. 8; *Indianapolis Star,* December 16, 1937, p. 10; *Christian Century* 55, (January 5, 1938), p. 8.

[34] *Manchester Guardian,* January 12, 1938, p. 8; *The Economist* (London), 131 (January 15, 1938), 106; Nicholas Halasz, *Roosevelt Through Foreign Eyes* (Princeton: D. Van Nostrand Co., Inc., 1961), p. 108.

[35] *The Times* (London), December 29, 1937, p. 9.

[36] *Washington Post,* January 10, 1938, p. 7.

[37] *Literary Digest,* 125, (January 1, 1938), 7; U.S., *Congressional Record,* 75th Cong., 3rd Sess., 1938, LXXXIII, Part 9, Appendix, 64, 97.

[38] House, Committee on the Judiciary, Ludlow Referendum, 75th Cong., 3rd Sess., NA, LD; *Literary Digest,* 125 (January 1, 1938), 7.

[39] Ludlow Referendum, OF 3084, Roosevelt Papers; *Literary Digest,* 125 (January 1, 1938), 7.

[40] *New York Times,* December 19, 1937, p. 8.

[41] *Ibid.,* December 22, 1937, p. 24.

[42] *Literary Digest* 125 (January 1, 1938), 7.

[43] *Ibid.; New York Times,* January 10, 1938, p. 1; U.S., *Congressional Record,* 75th Cong., 3rd Sess., 1938, LXXXIII, Part 9, 165.

[44] *Congressional Digest,* 17 (February, 1938), 63; Radio Address by A. D. McReynolds, December 28, 1937. Cordell Hull Papers, Manuscript Division, Library of Congress. Cited hereafter as Hull Papers.

[45] Ludlow Referendum, OF 3084, Roosevelt Papers.

[46] Cordell Hull, *The Memoirs of Cordell Hull* (New York: The Macmillan Co., 1948), I, 564.

[47] *Christian Science Monitor,* December 21, 1937, p. 1.

[48] U. S. *Congressional Record,* 75th Cong., 3rd Sess., 1938, LXXXIII, Part 9, Appendix, 126-127.

[49] *Ibid.,* 277; see also *Roosevelt's Foreign Policy 1933-1941* (New York: Wilfred Funk Inc., 1942), p. 137.

[50] Divine, p. 49; U.S., Department of State, *Public Attitude Studies* (Washington: GPO 1941), p. 74.

[51] *San Francisco Chronicle,* January 12, 1938, p. 10; *Des Moines Register,* January 12, 1938, p. 6; *New York Times,* January 11, 1938, p. 22.

[52] Elliott Roosevelt (ed.), *F.D.R. His Personal Letters, 1928-1945* (New York: Duell, Sloan and Pearce, 1950), II, 751.

CHAPTER V

NAVAL EXPANSION

The United States Navy was considered a vast and complex instrument of force designed to protect the nation and wage a successful war on the sea, if called upon. The fleet, which was the concrete embodiment of this force, was built in accordance with the requirements of well-defined plans to secure victory when the occasion arose. But American naval policies and plans during the decade after 1919 were, for the most part, influenced by a strong isolationist movement which had engulfed the nation at that time. This pacifist outlook was also instrumental in determining American policy during the subsequent naval conferences which were held between the major powers following the First World War. The Washington Naval Conference, called in 1921-1922 by Secretary of State Charles Evans Hughes, was the first of such meetings which attempted to limit the size and strength of the ranking world navies. At this conference, the United States sought naval parity with Great Britain while at the same time it hoped to curb Japanese naval expansion. Ostensibly, the American effort proved successful when the representatives from Great Britain, the United States, Japan, France, and Italy signed the so-called Five Power Treaty of naval limitations (see Appendix I). The major terms of the treaty provided for:

1. The establishment of a 5:5:3 ratio between the United States, Great Britain and Japan respectively in capital ship strength.
2. A ten-year halt in the construction of capital ships and scrapping of all uncompleted vessels.
3. After ten years the building of replacements might begin and older vessels would be scrapped as replacements are completed.
4. No ship to exceed 35,000 tons in displacement or carry guns of more than a 16-inch bore.
5. Treaty to remain in force until 31 December 1936 and thereafter subject to a two-year notice of termination by any one of the signatories.[1]

Under these provisions, the United States scrapped a greater amount of future tonnage than the other signatories. Specifically, Hughes agreed to halt the proposed construction of 28 battleships and battlecruisers. But the Five Power Treaty was considered from the American standpoint as a diplomatic victory. The treaty enabled the United States to attain naval equality in capital ship construction with Great Britain and a five-to-three naval superiority over Japan, in addition to eliminating the burdens of costly expenditures in this category. The settlement, nevertheless, failed to limit the construction of other ships, such as cruisers, destroyers and submarines, which had not been considered vital at the time. Between 1922 and 1927, both Great Britain and Japan threatened to upset the 5:5:3 balance established at the Washington Conference when they embarked upon the construction of these auxiliary vessels. In the summer of 1927, President Calvin Coolidge called upon the other ranking naval powers to meet in Geneva in order to solve the dilemma surrounding the building of subsidiary craft. The Geneva meeting, unlike the Washington Conference six years earlier, ended in total failure. France and Italy refused to send representatives to the conference, while the United States and Great Britain reached an impasse over the issue of cruiser displacement. The British wanted parity only in capital vessels whereas the United States insisted upon equality in all categories.[2]

The change of administrations in both countries by 1929 cleared the way for a rapprochement on Anglo-American naval problems and a new conference was summoned for the following year in London. As it turned out, the London Conference of 1930 was the last successful effort to limit naval expansion by diplomatic action. The conflicts which had terminated the Geneva Conference were quickly eliminated. The 5:5:3 ratio was established in most categories between the United States, Great Britain, and Japan, respectively, while Japan received a seven to ten ratio in destroyer and cruiser tonnage and parity in submarine displacement. France and Italy also attended the meeting but the disparity shown in regard to their ratios of auxiliary vessels led their delegates to concur only upon part of the agreement. (See Appendix I).[3]

The period of relative naval harmony was ended a year later when Japan invaded Manchuria. Japanese militarists, who had always considered the inferior naval status as an affront to their power and prestige, now sought naval equality with the United States and Great Britain. In 1934, Japan informed the signatories of the Five Power Treaty of her intention to withdraw from the agreement by December 31, 1936. Methods of ironing out these difficulties were attempted at a subsequent conference in London in 1935-1936, but the Japanese representatives withdrew immediately when their demands for naval equality in all categories were rejected by the other powers. Several agreements, however, were reached at the conference between the United States, Great Britain, and France. The total amount of tonnage in each category was lifted, but the three powers agreed that the size of battleships would be restricted to 35,000 tons and with a gun bore of 14 inches instead of the 16 inches which had been allocated under the provisions of the Washington Treaty.* Each signatory further agreed to notify the others concerning additional naval construction. An escalator clause was also provided which released any member from these restrictions upon specific evidence that other nations were exceeding the tonnage in capital ship construction.[4]

It was during this period of limitations, treaties, and ratios that opinion on American naval policy developed into four distinct categories. The most powerful and influential group were the isolationists who maintained that the two oceans provided an assured safeguard against invasion and therefore a navy powerful enough merely to protect the American trade routes would be adequate. This sentiment was prevalent particularly in the Middle West and other inland sections of the country. The second group consisted of the so-called "treaty-navy" faction which held strictly to the limits established by the naval treaties. They believed that the present American naval ratio was sufficient for defensive purposes. The third group embodied the "navy second to none" theory in which they advocated nothing less than equal parity with Great Britain. The fourth faction, on the other hand, adhered to the policy of supremacy on the sea. This group, which was to dominate American naval thinking in the future, believed that universal peace would be established through the leadership of a dominant sea power; the United States, they felt, was the only nation capable of assuming this leadership due to the nation's geographical position and wealth of resources. Roosevelt hoped that the United States eventually would become the ranking naval power in the world, but in the meantime, he supported the policy of a navy second to none.[5]

When the Japanese invaded China in July, 1937, Roosevelt was suddenly faced with the two-fold possibility that the war might upset the status quo in China and that the American island

---

* The signatories assented, however, to a six-year holiday in the construction of heavy cruisers.

possessions in the Pacific might be in jeopardy if hostilities moved southward. In either case, the President and his secretary of state were convinced that Japan now loomed as the greatest threat to the balance of power in the Far East. One possible solution to this threat centered upon expanding the American Navy to the very limits established at the Washington and London Conferences. A strong naval force, Roosevelt felt, would serve as an effective deterrent to possible Japanese encroachments in the Pacific and would afford protection to American vital interests there. But he fully realized that a program of naval expansion at this time would meet with opposition from an isolationist Congress and the general public which would consider such a move as tantamount to war. This attitude was reflected in the uncertain reaction to his quarantine speech in Chicago on October 5, 1937. Nevertheless, Roosevelt continued to expound privately upon the necessity for a larger navy, although he was aware that many in Congress still remained fearful that a future war in the Pacific was possible.[6]

Two factors, occurring within days of each other, helped to pave the way for Roosevelt in his plans to increase the navy. The Japanese attack upon the *Panay* and the subsequent diplomatic crisis it produced had convinced the President and the State Department that specific measures must be formulated to counter any future Japanese violation upon American rights and interests. The second factor involved a newspaper story published on December 20, 1937, in the *Giornale d'Italia* of Rome which indicated that Japan had a total of 294,640 tons of new naval vessels under construction. This total went beyond what was officially known by the State Department of Japanese naval building since their withdrawal from the London Conference in December, 1935. With this new construction, the Japanese would have a total fleet tonnage of 1,119,000 in contrast to the American total of 1,418,895 tons. Though the United States still remained ahead of Japan in total tonnage, it was a narrower margin than the 5:5:3 ratio established at the Washington Conference. American naval experts considered the margin as critical since the distribution of capital ships in the Japanese Navy would be much higher upon completion of its program. More important, however, the newspaper article indicated that the new Japanese naval program included three super-battleships of 45,000 tons each and mounting twelve 16-inch guns; further that these ships violated the provisions established by the London Naval Treaty of 1936 limiting capital vessels to 35,000 tons. The United States had observed the 35,000 ton limit when the *USS North Carolina* and the *USS Washington* were con-

structed in early 1937. Roosevelt and officials from the State and
Navy Departments reportedly considered the newspaper article as
genuine, since it had been published in the semi-official Italian
newspaper following Italy's endorsement of the Anti-Comintern
Pact.[7]

The President now sought ways to meet the growing problems
in the Far East. In a letter dated December 28, 1937, to Edward
T. Taylor, chairman of the House Appropriations Committee,
Roosevelt inquired about the possibility of expanding naval construction. In making the request, he did not refer to any particular nation or to any specific threat against the United States,
although the Japanese buildup weighed heavily in his determination to increase the size of the navy. Taylor informed the President
that the 1938-1939 naval budget would provide for the construction of two battleships, two light cruisers, eight destroyers and six
submarines. Taylor also asserted that since the United States
had built, or was in the process of building, aircraft carriers at
least equal in number to those of any other power "it is not necessary at this time to commence the construction of airplane carriers."[8] Roosevelt believed that the 1938-1939 naval budget was
inadequate for what he termed defensive purposes and on December 29, 1937, he announced at a press conference that a larger
naval program would be given to Congress, although he did not
reveal what specific increases were contemplated. "The general
international picture," he told the press, "has made it possible
for the laying down of additional vessels besides those that were
provided for in the budget."[9]

On January 5, 1938, Roosevelt met with Admiral Leahy and
Carl Vinson, chairman of the House Naval Affairs Committee,
to determine what increases would be requested from Congress.
All three believed that if the United States were to maintain its
naval strength in comparison to other nations, the 1938-1939 program would have to be expanded to include two additional battleships and two light cruisers. Plans were now made to increase
the total tonnage of the navy by 20 percent above the limit
established by the Vinson-Trammell Naval Act of 1934 which
restricted the United States Navy in size according to the London treaty of 1930.[10]

In his annual message to Congress early in January, 1938,
Roosevelt initiated his new armament campaign when he stressed
the need for keeping "adequately strong in self-defense." On
January 21, Congress complied and passed the 1938-1939 naval

budget of $547 million in order to continue the completion of vessels currently under construction; at the same time Congress approved the building of two battleships, two light cruisers, eight destroyers, six submarines, and several other minor vessels.[11] Then on January 28, Roosevelt, in a special message to Congress, suddenly recommended a far reaching additional naval expansion program. This new naval program, separate and distinct from the annual naval budget passed recently by the lawmakers, called for:

1. Twenty percent expansion of the fleet to 46 warships or 618,082 tons.
2. Authorization for 26 auxiliaries including submarines, destroyers, and seaplane tenders totaling 182,250 tons.
3. A 50 percent increase in naval aircraft from 1,910 to 3,000.
4. An additional 1,025 line officers.
5. An immediate appropriation to begin two additional battleships and two additional light cruisers above the estimates for the current fiscal year 1938-1939.
6. An immediate appropriation of $15 million for new types of small experimental fighting ships.[12]

No nation was named precisely by the President as the cause for recommending further naval expansion, but by all indications it appeared that the increases which he requested were aimed partly at Japan and the possibility of a two-ocean war. He assured Congress, however, that the expanded navy would be employed for defensive purposes only and not for intervention overseas.

> We cannot assume that our defense would be limited to one ocean and one coast and that the other ocean and the other coast would with certainty be safe. Adequate defense, therefore, affects the simultaneous defense of every part of the United States. This is the purpose of these recommendations. Such protection is and will be based not on aggression but on defense.[13]

On the same day, Carl Vinson introduced a bill in Congress endorsing all of the President's proposals. To quell any questions as to the purpose of the naval increases, a section was inserted into the Second Vinson Naval Bill which stated:

> The fundamental naval policy of the United States is to maintain an adequate navy in sufficient strength to guard the Continental United States by affording naval protection to the coast line in both oceans at one and the same time; to protect the Panama Canal, Alaska, Hawaii and our insular possessions; to protect our commerce and citizens abroad; to maintain a navy in sufficient strength; to guarantee our national security but not for aggression; to insure our national integrity and to support our national policies.[14]

The proposed naval expansion bill was immediately attacked by isolationists who declared that the measure was the practical extension of Roosevelt's quarantine policy; a move which they felt would embroil the nation ultimately in another war. Opponents of the bill, such as Nye, Borah, and Vandenberg, claimed that the alleged increase was not intended for defensive purposes but rather it was an attempt by Roosevelt to shift American foreign policy and undertake a more active role in the Far East. Other critics felt that the naval buildup was closely linked with the recent incident over the *Panay*.[15]

Editorial opinion over the proposed increases was sharply divided, although newspapers along the Pacific and Atlantic coasts generally favored the measure. One of the major newspapers in the East which criticized Roosevelt's program was the *New York Herald Tribune* which viewed the naval program as a heavy economic burden "without the slightest explanation of the basic policy which it is intended to fulfill." The *Herald Tribune* advocated a thorough re-evaluation of American defensive positions before such intensive arms construction was initiated. The *Newark Evening News* refused to support the program since no effective reason had been offered to necessitate the enormous authorization. The newspaper editorial stated that the naval increase was aimed only at protecting American interests in the Far East. The *Baltimore Sun* was hesitant in approving the increases when it maintained in an editorial that the over-age vessels currently under repair, in addition to the vessels scheduled for construction, "would find our navy not only with more than twice as many ships as we now have but also twice as many men."[16]

The *Birmingham News,* in commenting on the increases, was as critical of naval construction as it was of the world armament race which it believed had influenced the Administration. Nevertheless, the newspaper editorial urged the government to pause and consider the consequences of augmenting naval expenditures at this time. The *Cincinnati Inquirer* bitterly criticized the theory that the United States should possess a navy second to none. "It would be a tragic farce," the editorial warned, "if the *Panay* incident were to plunge the American people into a ruinous armaments race." The newspaper editorial pointed out that the United States Navy was still considered vastly superior to the Japanese Navy and quite capable of defending American shores if an attack occurred. The isolationist *Omaha World Herald* stated editorially that naval expansion would lead ultimately to war. The *World Herald* supported the theory that war would bring profiteers and ". . . this democracy will become, in practice at least, a stern fascist state." Anticipating the naval program, a *Des Moines Register* editorial attacked such a proposal and saw no compelling reason for enlarging the navy. The newspaper editorial asserted that the increases were really intended to counter a Japanese naval threat and added that if war came, "it could not be won since it would be fought in Japanese waters thousands of miles from our coasts." The *Minneapolis Tribune* criticized Roosevelt's proposal for naval increases when the editorial writer remarked that "the arms program is more a move in the international chess game of a war-minded diplomacy than it is an effort at meeting an open threat against national Security." A *Butte Standard* (Montana) editorial did not favor the naval building program, asserting that it was not "necessary, sound or logical for us to match ship for ship, gun for gun, and man for man with the mad-dog governments of the world." The *Arizona Republic* doubted the necessity of establishing naval supremacy which Roosevelt appeared to advocate. The *Republic* urged the government to act only as a bystander in the naval armament race with Japan. "Nor do we think," the newspaper editorial stated, "that Japan's oblique way of thinking will be carried to such an extent as to bring these two nations into armed conflict."[17]

Several magazines also opposed Roosevelt's proposed plan for naval expansion. In an editorial comment, the *Christian Century* ostensibly believed the construction of a super navy rested on the premise that it would challenge the belligerent actions of Japan. The magazine predicted that such a program would "precipitate the most suicidal naval building race ever known." The *Christian Century* further believed that naval increases were based in part on economic factors. Since the nation was currently involved in a depression, the magazine editorial asserted that Roosevelt was attempting to stimulate business through an enormous outlay of federal spending. *Scholastic* magazine retorted in an editorial that the only reason for a large navy was to serve in conjunction with a foreign policy geared toward embroiling the United States in a war with Japan. The magazine believed that Roosevelt was systematically carrying out the plans which he had disclosed in his quarantine speech in Chicago in October, 1937. The isolationist *New Republic* remarked caustically that the President wanted more vessels before the next *Panay* incident occurred "so that a vast American armada can steam across the Pacific and blow up the Japanese island."[18]

Various peace organizations immediately indicated their opposition to Roosevelt's naval increases. Frederick J. Libby, executive secretary of the National Council for the Prevention of War, declared that the naval program was based upon a foreign policy which would lead the United States into war. With the *Panay* incident in mind, Estelle M. Sternberger, executive director of World Peaceways, believed that "our navy must be built for home defense only and not for extricating us from embarrassing situations abroad." Norman Thomas, chairman of the Socialist Party, in commenting on the naval progress to the press declared:

> This tremendous expenditure is the first step toward an Anglo-American alliance in which through joint naval action the battle fleets of America and Great Britain will attempt to roll up the Japanese navy. Do so and we will get a totalitarian state.[19]

Although many newspapers had opposed naval increases, more newspapers editorially expressed their approval for Roosevelt's plan to expand the navy. As early as December 30, 1937, the *New York Times* endorsed any program for naval increases. "Additional building on our part," the newspaper editorial remarked, "is now required for the purpose of upholding American prestige in a world in which nations have come to respect force and force alone." Other newspapers along the eastern seaboard also favored naval expansion. With an eye towards a possible invasion from the Atlantic, the *Boston Globe* gave its support for a two-ocean navy and warned any European nation to take note that the naval bill would strengthen the Monroe Doctrine in both hemispheres. A *Providence Journal* editorial indicated that it would be sheer folly for the government not to spend adequate sums for the defense of the nation and urged Congress to approve the program. The *Philadelphia Inquirer* justified the increases when it declared in an editorial that "if up-building our national defenses on a scale never before deemed necessary evinces a lack of faith in the future of world peace, this is not America's fault. The blame belongs not to this nation, but to those powers openly aiming at aggression."[20]

Further inland, the *Buffalo Evening News* supported the program and maintained that American armaments were inadequate when compared to other naval powers. Such a plan, the newspaper editorial pointed out, would "discourage nations contemplating aggression from attacking a country which would not be defenseless." The *Pittsburgh Post-Gazette* contended that the current world situation had made it necessary for the government to defend the nation's rights. Although the newspaper predicted that isolationists in Congress would attempt to defeat the measure, "there should be no hesitancy about making whatever increases are shown to be necessary." The *Cleveland Plain Dealer* backed the President in his call for a larger navy, while a *Detroit Free Press* editorial explained that Roosevelt's program was not excessive, but a plan which would provide a force sufficient enough to counter any threats upon the Western Hemisphere. "The only way to prevent an attack," the editorial added, "is to build and maintain a navy strong enough to keep any enemy from Asia or Europe from coming within striking distance of our shores by water or air."[21]

In the South, the *Richmond Times-Dispatch* voiced its approval for the naval program and asserted that the measure "should create the proper psychological atmosphere in the international realm by giving the gangster governments clear evidence that the United States has not gone completely isolationist." The *New Orleans Times-Picayune* offered its full support to the naval program while the *Nashville Banner* maintained in an editorial that world conditions had caused the United States to enter the naval race. "It is in meeting this changing condition," the newspaper editorial remarked, "and with understandable reluctance that America enters the naval race."[22]

In the Midwest, where isolationist sentiment was generally strongest, many newspapers, nevertheless, supported naval expansion. The *Indianapolis Star* favored the measure as a check to ambitious dictators and added that American influence in international affairs depended largely upon the strength of its navy. The *St. Louis Post-Dispatch,* like the *Nashville Banner,* believed that the proposed naval bill came as a result of world conditions and in an editorial predicted that Congress and the public would approve the increases. Two of Chicago's largest newspapers expressed their approval for Roosevelt's naval program. The conservative *Chicago Tribune* advocated a stronger navy as early as December 18, 1937, especially one more powerful and larger than the Japanese Navy. With the failure of the naval limitation treaties, the *Tribune* vigorously urged the government not to delay in the construction of more vessels. The more liberal *Chicago Daily News* took a similar viewpoint, particularly in light of the Japanese refusal to uphold the naval treaties. "We know now," the *Daily News* editorial remarked, "what we could not possibly have known then, namely, that an agreement made with Japan is valueless." The *Milwaukee Journal* favored the big navy when it maintained that the navy must be large enough "not only to protect our coasts but to keep an enemy many hundreds of miles away from our continental limits."[23]

Most newspapers along the Pacific coast favored plans for naval expansion since they feared that if a future war with Japan occurred, the Far Western area of the United States might be threatened directly. The *Salt Lake City Tribune* urged the government not to "shirk its duty to protect its people and institutions from insults and assaults from land and sea." The *Albuquerque Journal* believed that a larger navy was needed "so that we will keep pace with the other great powers." Following the settlement of the *Panay* episode, the *Los Angeles Times* supported moves toward naval expansion. "As matters stand," a *Times* editorial stated, "our best assurance of peace will come from being strong enough that we cannot be attacked successfully." In commenting editorially on the naval program, the *Sacramento Union* announced that the measure would "give notice to aggressor nations that this country is moving to prepare itself against any eventuality." The *San Francisco Chronicle* admitted that Roosevelt's program for naval expansion had become imperative since the *Panay* crisis. "We are neither imperialistic nor militaristic," the *Chronicle* editorial declared, "but we must be prudent. We cannot by weakness invite attack." The *Portland Oregonian* took a more philosophical attitude when it remarked in an editorial that naval increases "are fully justified on the basis of things as they actually are in the world rather than on things as they should be." Roosevelt's naval building program received unanimous support from several newspapers in Washington such as the *Seattle Daily Times, Hoquiam Washingtonian, Olympia News* and the *Yakima Herald*. Normally an isolationist-oriented magazine, the *Scientific American* sustained the President's plan for naval increases and added that the *Panay* incident had proven that the American public had been awakened out of its complacency. "We want a return," the magazine editorial declared, "to the traditional principle that our flag must be respected wherever flown."[24]

The noted newspaper columnist, Walter Lippmann, favored Roosevelt's naval proposal and asserted that with the world in disorder, the American Navy should be made stronger. Lippmann pointed to the *Panay* crisis in which he felt that American influence and prestige had been momentarily lost and therefore he called for "a great navy in order to insure a decent respect for our interests."[25]

With a view toward a possible Anglo-American naval alliance, newspapers in Great Britain welcomed and approved of Roosevelt's naval building program. The *Times* (London) considered American naval rearmament as a move aimed at world security, while the *Economist* (London) believed that Japanese naval expansion would now be checked effectively by the American naval increases. The *London Observor* was particularly critical of the Japanese intention to destroy the naval balance. "By refusing to cooperate with other nations and by insisting upon a common upper limit," the *Observor* editorial indicated, "Japan is imposing a burden upon all mankind."[26]

The European attitude toward American naval expansion was based on the belief that Roosevelt's plans were influenced by the Far Eastern situation in general and the *Panay* incident in particular. Indeed, it was believed that any American move to stem Japanese hegemony in the Pacific tended to impede upon the policies of Germany and Italy since it would add to British naval power. Hence, any American proposal to strengthen its naval forces would be contrary to the ultimate aims of the Axis powers. Hans H. Dieckhoff, the German Ambassador to the United States, anticipated a change in American foreign policy when he informed his government on January 3, 1938, following Roosevelt's annual message to Congress, that the American President was pursuing a policy against complete isolation. Dieckhoff was convinced that Roosevelt would undertake a program of greater preparedness, specifically in regard to naval increases.[27] When Roosevelt recommended the plans to expand the navy on January 28, the German press as a whole severely criticized the move. The newspaper *Lokalanzeiger,* summarized German reaction when it asserted in an editorial that the United States was currently gripped by a war psychosis which would silence opponents to the Vinson bill. The German Admiral Franz W. Brueninghaus, on the other hand, felt that the naval buildup was aimed instead at America's traditional competitor Great Britain. Brueninghaus disclaimed any German responsibility for the increases and attributed the renewed naval program to Anglo-Saxon negligence. At the same time, he believed Japan's efforts to expand its navy were "in order for an island power to safeguard her supplies."[28]

On the other side of the world, Japanese officials and the press were annoyed and critical of Roosevelt's naval expansion plan since they felt that it was directed against Japan. In an editorial, the *Tokyo Asahi* questioned the validity of the program as a defensive measure and added that the increases would force Japan "by the necessity of considering adequate counter-measures to cope with the new developments." A *Japan Times and Mail* editorial maintained that the American building program would endanger world peace while it categorically denied any intentions on the part of Japan to enter a naval race. "Any Japanese naval construction," the editorial contended, "is meant only to defend herself against all possible emergencies." The *Tokyo Nichi Nichi* voiced a similar opinion in an editorial asserting that both the United States and Great Britain were interfering with Japan's right to defend itself. The *Miyako* maintained that Anglo-Saxon powers were attempting to exploit Japan in order to find a pretext for naval expansion. The *Tokyo Yoimuri* pointed out in an editorial that if the United States and Great Britain had approved of the Japanese request for a common upper limit in tonnage during the London Conference of 1936, the current naval race would never have occurred.[29]

Several officials in Japan viewed the American increase mixed with feelings of indignation and regret. Mitsumasa Yonai, the Japanese Navy Minister, told a plenary session of the Diet on February 1 that Japan had no intention of maintaining naval parity with the United States and Great Britain despite naval construction by these two nations. War Minister General Sugiyama was nevertheless convinced that Japan would be forced to expand its armaments as a result of increases by other powers. He later told the press:

> In view of the expansion of armaments by other countries, it will be unavoidable for Japan also to increase her armaments and the government will take the proper measures according to future developments.

Several ranking Japanese naval officers felt certain that Roosevelt's objective in pursuing a big navy was intended for an eventual clash with Japan in the Pacific. Speaking for the navy, Rear-Admiral Tota Ishimaru considered the Japanese Navy far superior in quality to the American fleet at that time, although he believed that a future war against the combined navies of the West would be perilous to Japan.[30]

Almost immediately following Roosevelt's announced plans to expand the navy, the State Department attempted to learn whether Japan had constructed or was in the process of constructing capital ships of 45,000 tons each. On February 4, Hull instructed Joseph C. Grew to obtain this information and to remind Koki Hirota, the Japanese Foreign Minister, that according to the provisions of the London Naval Treaty of 1936, the construction of vessels exceeding the 35,000-ton limit was expressly prohibited. In a note to Hirota on the following day, Grew asked whether the Japanese government intended to adhere to the agreement since reports indicated that it was constructing vessels in excess of the treaty limitations. The American ambassador asserted that unless the Japanese government furnished assurances to the contrary, the United States would invoke the escalator clause of the London Treaty and would begin the building of 45,000-ton vessels. Grew requested a reply no later than February 20 and if no reply were received or if the reply lacked the intended assurances, the United States would then presume that the Japanese government was constructing the super-battleships. Negotiations were left open, nevertheless, when Grew declared that if the Japanese revealed the tonnages and gun calibers of its vessels, the American government would be willing to discuss the question of limitations in these areas at a conference.[31]

The Japanese press immediately questioned the temerity of the American request concerning tonnage limitations and maintained that Japan, which had never been a party to the London Conference of 1936, had every right to refuse such assurances to the Western powers. The *Japan Times and Mail* summed up editorial reaction to the issue when it reiterated:

> Japan will give due consideration to the naval strength of other nations but will never join a useless construction race. We are determined to protect ourselves with a navy suitable to the peculiar conditions and characteristics of the country.[32]

Hirota replied to the American ambassador on February 12 "that the mere communication of information concerning the construction of vessels will not contribute to any fair and equitable measure of disarmament and I regret that I am unable to comply with the desire of your government on this point." In other words, the foreign minister flatly refused to divulge any knowledge as to whether Japan was constructing vessels of 45,000 tons. Hirota also rejected Grew's proposal for a conference on future limitations since qualitative restrictions, if not accompanied by quantitative restrictions, would favor the United States. Hirota told Grew, however, that his government would consider a future conference on quantitative limitations if Japan received equal parity with Great Britain and the United States in capital ship construction.[33]

The secretary of state viewed the Japanese proposal for quantitative reduction as an effort to freeze the construction of the American and British fleets at their present level while Japan continued to build its navy up to the level of both the United

States and Great Britain. Hence, Hull regarded the Japanese willingness to discuss quantitative and not qualitative limitations simply as another bid for naval equality with the West. Nor was the secretary of state pleased with the unwillingness of the Japanese government to disclose any information concerning the construction of 45,000-ton vessels. Hull was convinced that the Japanese secrecy surrounding the building of such ships would merely "encourage rather than discourage an armaments race."[34] Roosevelt was also opposed to giving Japan naval parity since the United States "might have to meet an attack simultaneously on both the Atlantic and the Pacific." At a press conference, the President declared that if Japan were allowed naval parity, the United States could not meet Japan on equal terms in the Pacific in the event of an attack on both coasts. But if the 5:5:3 ratio were maintained, Roosevelt felt certain that the United States could dispatch at least 40 percent of its fleet to the Pacific and still oppose Japan with an equal force.[35]

With no assurances given by Japan on the question of 45,000-ton battleships, Hull informed the British government that the United States would exercise the right given under the provisions of the London Treaty of 1936 to depart from further limitations and restrictions and begin construction of 45,000-ton vessels. By April 1, 1938, the escalator clause was invoked by the remaining signatories to the treaty; they were now free to construct capital ships exceeding the 35,000-ton limit.[36]

During the ensuing months following Roosevelt's recommendations for naval expansion, Congressional hearings and debates were held to determine the necessity for such an enormous increase. In the House, Carl Vinson defended the naval expansion bill almost immediately after the President's special message to Congress on January 28. He told House members that Japan and Great Britain no longer limited their navies to the 5:5:3 ratio established at the Washington and London Conferences while the United States continued under the prescribed ratio. In proposing the bill, Vinson explained that its passage would enable the nation to attain its rightful place among the major naval powers of the world and would prevent any potential attack upon the United States and its insular possessions. The Georgia Democrat attempted to assure isolationists in Congress that the expansion program was not intended for offensive purposes but rather as a quarantine for the United States against external attack.

> We have no desire to police the world. We are not building the Navy to get entangled in any alien quarrels. This bill is not here

for the purpose of building a navy to make China and Japan or any other nation safe for democracy. It is here for the purpose of insuring peace for America.[37]

Vinson further assured doubting congressmen that the United States was not collaborating with Great Britain in some form of a naval alliance or agreement. Hull reiterated this policy in a letter to Louis Ludlow when he asserted that at the present time "the proposed naval enlargement program does not contemplate the use of the units in cooperation with any other nation in any part of the world." Even Ludlow favored any proposal which might strengthen the American Navy. As early as January 9, 1938, he told the press that "I shall vote for naval expansion . . . which would cause warring nations to think twice before attacking us but I regret it that other nations force us to do it."[38]

Many congressmen, nevertheless, refused to believe that naval expansion underscored a policy of defense which pro-navy men had consistently maintained. Hamilton Fish, the ranking Republican member on the House Committee on Foreign Affairs, opposed any plan for naval increases as "unnecessary for defense and inconsistent with our foreign policies of keeping out of European and Asiatic blood feuds and conflicts." Fish was convinced that the naval program would merely serve as an encouragement to further aggression, while at the same time it would add to Roosevelt's determination to police the world. Maury Maverick of Texas believed that the present naval superiority over Japan was adequate to stop any possibility of an attack by the Asiatic power. With the recent *Panay* incident still in mind, John W. Robsion of Kentucky felt that the naval bill would give Roosevelt "or any captain of any American vessel" the opportunity to involve the United States in a war.[39]

In opposing the naval rearmament program, Henry C. Luckey of Nebraska outlined the disadvantages of such an undertaking.

1. It is not necessary from the standpoint of actual national defense.
2. It places the country in the leadership of the world naval race.
3. It intensifies international rivalries instead of encouraging good will among nations.
4. It propels us into Asiatic and European power politics.
5. It weakens our national defense by extending our defense line beyond the Western Hemisphere.

Luckey felt that Japan would never attack the United States since its interests centered in the Far East. "Not even the most fool-hardy nation," he told his colleagues, "would attack a far more powerful nation upon its own ground unless there was a considerable prospect of success."[40]

Ralph O. Brewster of Maine opposed the increase in naval appropriations and maintained that it was an attempt by the Administration to entangle the nation in power politics. Brewster advocated a greater enforcement of the Neutrality Act by stopping the shipment of munitions and essential war materials to Japan. Harold Knutson of Minnesota reiterated a similar attitude when he declared that the proposed naval buildup was designed "to increase our naval strength to a point where we can enforce our will in the Orient and Europe." Knutson believed that the navy was large enough to defend the Western Hemisphere and if necessary American possessions overseas.[41]

Not all congressmen, however, disapproved of a larger peacetime navy. Charles A. Wolverton of New Jersey impressed upon House members that the naval increases would serve as a containment against aggression. He pointed to the present war in China which he felt was "the consequence of a short-sighted policy upon China's part to provide for adequate defense." The New Jersey congressman firmly believed that an insufficient navy would inevitably invite attack from potential aggressors.[42] Supporting the Vinson bill, James W. Mott of Oregon reassured doubtful congressmen that the proposed authorization was instituted not with the intention of pursuing parallel action with other Western powers. The bill originated, he explained, as a result of Japan's repudiation of the 5:5:3 ratio as outlined by previous naval treaties. Mott also indicated that Japan was constructing 45,000-ton battleships which were larger than any capital vessel the United States possessed at that time. He warned his colleagues:

> If we should get into a foreign war, we must protect ourselves; we cannot look for protection to any other country; and the only way we can protect ourselves is to have a navy big enough and strong enough to prevent any foreign power from reaching our shores. . . . It is the best insurance for peace and the cheapest insurance against war that we can possibly get.[43]

John L. McClellan of Arkansas, like Robsion, also had the *Panay* episode in mind, but he asserted that there would be less danger of surprise attack if naval preparations were undertaken. Alfred N. Phillips offered his support for the bill, and told House members that the comparative length of the American and Japanese coasts indicated an imperative need for a larger American Navy of defense. According to Phillips, the total distance of the Pacific and Atlantic coasts, including the coastlines of

Puerto Rico, Alaska, and Hawaii, was 9,600 miles as opposed to 4,190 miles of coastline around Japan, the Kuril Islands, Taiwan and the Nansei Islands. These differences, Phillips maintained, did not include Central and South America whose coastlines totaled 15,640 miles. The Connecticut congressman believed that the proposed naval increases would still fall short in providing ample naval protection to the Western Hemisphere in the event of an attack.[44]

While debate on the issue continued, the House Naval Affairs Committee headed by Vinson conducted hearings to air both the advantages and disadvantages for naval expansion. Admiral Leahy summarized the arguments for the increases when he told the committee that the navy must be maintained continually to guard the nation's vital interests against an attack by any nation or group of nations. The chief of naval operations attempted to dispell any misgivings brought out during the course of the hearings that the bill was a device to render military assistance to Great Britain; he indicated that the proposed increase was not intended to aid other nations. Nor was the expansion program, according to Leahy, directed against any one nation, such as Japan. He assured the committee on this point when he declared:

> The Navy must be prepared to provide defense against attack on our shores by any foreign power. In our preparations to carry out that duty we do not think of any particular foreign power but endeavor to make arrangements and to make provisions to repel an attack by any foreign navy.[45]

Leahy warned, however, that the bill would not produce a navy strong enough to counter a combination of enemy navies but rather it was geared to guard against only one major naval power. Leahy further maintained that fortifications along the Atlantic Coast were not sufficient to insure against a potential invasion. In the Pacific, Leahy contended that it would take approximately twice the number of vessels proposed in the increase to defend American possessions there.[46]

Appearing before the committee, the noted historian Charles A. Beard, took sharp issue with Roosevelt's naval program when he asserted that "the navy for which he asks could not assure the protection of our rights against the naval force of Japan." Beard pointed out that if the United States had a navy twice as large as Japan's, it still could not win a decisive battle in Far Eastern waters, nor could the navy offer substantial protection to American citizens in China. With the present Sino-Japanese conflict in mind, Beard urged an American withdrawal from foreign war zones and stated that the navy should not be employed "to protect the profits of traders in war-infested regions abroad."[47]

Various organizations, such as the National Council of Methodist Youth, the Woman's International League for Peace and Freedom, and the American League for Peace and Democracy, opposed the plan actively in open letters to the committee. The 24-member Naval Affairs Committee, however, approved the bill, although three Republicans and one Democrat, who had recommended its defeat, felt that the proposal would augment the quarantine theory which Roosevelt had outlined in his speech the preceeding October in Chicago. Nevertheless, on March 21, 1938, the House passed the new increase by a vote of 294-100 and the bill was submitted to the Senate for approval.[48]

Proponents of the bill were fully aware that a strong isolationist bloc in the upper chamber would attempt to oppose the program for naval expansion by claiming that the Administration was being deliberately exposed to the influences which brought about America's entry into the First World War. As one of the leading opponents of naval increases, Senator William E. Borah maintained that the current strength and size of the navy was sufficient to defend the nation; that the bill would only force the United States away from its traditional isolationist policy. According to Borah, the Administration was magnifying the impending dangers of a global war intentionally by proposing such a large naval rearmament program. He told Senate members:

> The Navy we have will be sufficient to protect our country if our Government remains at home. These combinations of powers of navies to cross the ocean and attack us seems to me without foundation in reason. They will all disappear after the bill is disposed of.

The Idaho senator dismissed thoughts of any future conflicts with Japan which naval exponents were predicting. "I do not think Japan wants war with the United States," he added, "and I do not think she is so situated that she could make war if she wanted to do so."[49] Borah reiterated this attitude in a letter to a constituent when he declared:

> Ever since I have been in the Senate, we have been building navies allegedly to fight Japan and now they are again citing Japan as a menace. There is, to my mind no probability of Japan attacking the United States. It is sheer folly to talk about it.[50]

Borah further nullified any suspicions that Japan was currently constructing 45,000-ton battleships. He impressed upon his colleagues that the building of such vessels was based entirely upon rumor, since no specific evidence was produced to indicate otherwise. Borah feared that if the United States embarked upon the construction of these super battleships it would initiate a naval race among the major powers in the world. Senator Arthur Vandenberg of Michigan supported Borah's contention on this issue and questioned the necessity for a large navy when in the preceeding 12 months neither Roosevelt nor the Navy Department found it essential to pursue naval expansion. "In the absence of any rational explanation for a sudden change," he declared, "I am unable to believe that the national security now requires that I shall suddenly commit my country to a billion dollar naval burden." Vandenberg further opposed the hypothesis advocated by the American Foreign Policy Association which had declared on February 11, 1938, ". . . that the Navy is in fact designed to serve as an active instrument of diplomacy in the present Far Eastern crisis." Under such a plan, according to the Michigan senator, naval policy would be controlled directly by the State Department. Vandenberg predicted that an American foreign policy sustained by an immense naval force would doubtlessly embroil the nation in every European and Far Eastern conflict.[51] Senator Rush K. Holt of West Virginia reiterated a similar contention by asserting that the proposed naval increase was an offensive rather than a defensive measure, a move which he professed would lead to war. In a press conference Holt declared:

> It is tragic that much of our foreign policy is dictated by men who are internationally minded. They are the self-same men who tried to lead us into the League of Nations. They are the self-same men who tried to slip us into the World Court. They are the self-same men who believe in collective security and foreign entanglements. Follow the advice of great leaders from George Washington down, by keeping ourselves clear of foreign entanglements.[52]

During the Senate debate, opponents of the bill suspected that the underlying motive behind naval expansion was a potential military alliance with Great Britain. Hiram Johnson of California subsequently proposed a resolution requesting specific information from the secretary of state as to whether any secret alliance existed or was contemplated with the Anglo-Saxon power. Hull answered this query in a letter to Key Pittman, chairman of the Senate Committee on Foreign Relations. The secretary assured Johnson and other isolationists that "we have no understanding or agreement expressed or implied, for the use of our Navy in conjunction with any other nation." Hull's assurances, however, did not satisfy isolationist senators like Nye and Borah who continued to maintain that the naval program was earmarked for a future alignment with Great Britain.[53]

Several isolationist senators ostensibly supported the recommendations for the naval program. Frederick Hale of Maine frankly admitted that a potential naval attack on the United States or its possessions was not unlikely and advocated a navy powerful enough to repel such an assault. Hale disclaimed any possibility that the bill would inaugurate a naval race among the powers. "The passage of this bill," he explained, "will do more to bring about a substantial world limitation on naval armaments than any other step we could take in this direction." Elbert D. Thomas of Utah, who had urged the government to "keep out of wars which do not concern us," believed that a large navy and army would serve this purpose. George W. Norris of Nebraska, who had been a long-standing opponent of a large navy, changed his views in light of world events. Commenting on the alleged construction of 45,000-ton battleships by Japan, he declared:

> I think there would be little chance for Japan to make any headway against our navy but she is . . . building battleships greater than any now in existence. She does not want them and does not need them except for conquest. We must, therefore, make reasonable preparations to meet such a contingency.[54]

Davis I. Walsh of Massachusetts, chairman of the Senate Naval Affairs Committee, described the program's advantages in detail during the debate on the issue. As the Senate's leading spokesman for naval increases, he pointed out that the United States must maintain no less than naval parity with Great Britain and a five to three ratio with Japan "since it will make war unlikely for us, will insure the well-being and prosperity of our people and will shorten any war we may be forced into." Walsh told Senate members that if the government constructed all the vessels authorized under the proffered plan the United States would only attain a 4.6 ratio. The percentage, he explained, would fall short of the goal for equality with Great Britain while Japan would forge ahead in the five to three ratio. The Massachusetts senator further assured opponents of naval expansion that:

1. The bill does not initiate a new and different foreign policy.
2. The bill is not for purposes of war but an insurance against war.
3. The bill is not proposed to expand naval strength in contemplation of any alliance, defensive or offensive with any nation.
4. The bill does not make the building of a single additional vessel mandatory. It does no more than authorize without time limit an expansion of our naval strength; that expansion cannot occur until the President calls on Congress for an appropriation and Congress votes the appropriation.

5. The bill sanctions the maintenance of our Navy at a level equal to the prevailing best.
6. The bill would limit construction to the 5:5:3 ratio.[55]

The Senate Naval Affairs Committee also conducted hearings on the proposed increases. Leahy again testified in favor of the bill and added that a navy capable only of defense would not be able to forestall a blockade of the United States or prevent the loss of American possessions overseas. Rexford L. Holmes, secretary of the National Patriotic Council, reiterated Leahy's viewpoint and in a detailed statement to the committee declared in part that "we must be prepared in advance to keep any potential enemy from our continental limits. Naval defense now is an absolute necessity, not after war comes." W. C. Hushing, national legislative representative of the American Federation of Labor, informed the committee that the AF of L and its affiliates favored increasing the navy. The Adequate Coast Defenses Association also supported the bill.[56]

Testifying against the naval expansion plan, retired Marine Corps General Smedley D. Butler favored the construction of small coastal defense vessels which he felt would effectively repel any potential invasion of American shores. "I propose to stay here," he remarked, "and do as they did at Bunker Hill . . . wait until you see the whites of their eyes." Thomas H. Healey, Dean of the School of Foreign Service at Georgetown University, believed that the American stake in the Far East was too insignificant to justify naval expansion. "I see no substantial reason," he told Committee members, "why the United States should become involved in the Far East as long as we mind our own business and do not go out of our way to start a war about matters which are of little concern to us." "No sound evidence of any sort," he added, "has been produced to show that a Japanese control of China, or even the Philippines, would be of any real danger to us."[57]

In letters to the committee, various organizations opposed the program for naval rearmament. The People's Lobby, The American Peace Movement, and the National Peace Conference regarded the increases as a step toward precipitating a costly arms race. The National Peace Conference, in particular, feared that Congress would be asked to fortify the Philippines and to establish more naval bases in Far Eastern waters if the bill were passed. But like its counterpart in the House, which had endorsed the bill earlier, the Senate committee by the end of April stamped its approval for the 20 percent increase in naval appropriations.[58]

One of the main criticisms by isolationists during the Senate debate on the bill centered upon the intended construction by the United States government of 45,000-ton battleships. Naval experts indicated to Senate members that the larger vessel would serve as a counterbalance to the alleged Japanese naval expansion. An amendment to the bill was nevertheless proposed on May 2, 1938, which provided "that no vessel in excess of 35,000 tons shall be laid down until the President has determined that a capital ship of a tonnage in excess of 35,000 tons has been officially projected, appropriated for, or laid down by another power." The modification to the bill was approved by a vote of 56-20 with 20 abstaining. Advocates who favored the super vessel viewed the amendment as a significant victory, since Japan neither affirmed nor denied the building of 45,000-ton battleships which enabled Roosevelt to embark upon the construction of vessels in this category. On May 3, 1938, the Senate passed the so-called Vinson-Trammell Naval bill by a vote of 56-28 with 12 abstaining. In the final vote, 49 Democrats and seven Republicans supported the measure; 17 Democrats, seven Republicans, two Farm-Laborites, one Independent and one Progressive opposed it. The additional costs to carry out the provisions of the Vinson-Trammell Naval bill over a period of years were as follows:

1.	46 combatant vessels*	$ 811,095,000
2.	26 auxiliary vessels	216,451,000
3.	950 airplanes	106,000,000
4.	Equipment and facilities at navy yards	8,000,000
5.	Expenditures for experimental purposes	15,000,000
	Total	$1,156,546,000[59]

The passage of the Vinson Bill enacted the largest peacetime naval appropriation to date. Yet, significantly, the United States was the last of the great naval powers to initiate a major new naval building program since Great Britain, Japan, Germany, and Italy had already begun to increase their navies beyond the prescribed limits established by the naval conferences. Pro-navy men like Roosevelt and Leahy were convinced that the ultimate remedy for navalism could be found in more navalism. Such an assumption was aimed in part at Japan, which was challenging American naval superiority by the spring of 1938. Ostensibly, naval expansion, coupled with the *Panay* episode earlier, marked a vital turning point in America's relations with Japan.[60]

---

* Vessels in this category included three battleships, two aircraft carriers, nine light cruisers, nine submarines, and 23 destroyers.

Notes

[1] George T. Davis, *A Navy Second to None* (New York: Harcourt, Brace & Co., 1940), pp. 277-278. Other excellent accounts of the Washington Conference are found in Raymond L. Buell, *The Washington Conference* (New York: D. Appleton & Co., 1922), pp. 52-53; Harold & Margaret Sprout, *Toward a New Order of Sea Power* (Princeton: Princeton University Press, 1940).

[2] Davis, pp. 535-539.

[3] Raymond G. O'Conner, *Perilous Equilibrium: The United States and the London Naval Conference of 1930* (Lawrence: University of Kansas Press, 1962), pp. 144-149.

[4] Davis, p. 539.

[5] *Current History*, 47 (May, 1938), 20.

[6] William L. Neumann, "How American Policy Toward Japan Contributed to War in the Pacific," *Perpetual War for Perpetual Peace: A Critical Examination of the Foreign Policy of Franklin D. Roosevelt and its Aftermath* ed. Harry E. Barnes, (Caldwell: Caxton Printers, Ltd., 1953), pp. 250-251; See also Charles A. Beard, *American Foreign Policy in the Making 1932-1940: A Study in Responsibilities* (New Haven: Yale University Press, 1946), p. 214.

[7] *Christian Science Monitor*, December 22, 1937, p. 4.

[8] Roosevelt to Taylor, December 28, 1937, OF 18, Franklin D. Roosevelt Papers, The Franklin D. Roosevelt Library, Hyde Park, N. Y. Cited hereafter as Roosevelt Papers.

[9] Press Conference, December 29, 1937, Roosevelt Papers. In a public opinion poll taken on December 28, 1937, 74 percent of those queried favored the construction of a larger navy. Hadley Cantril (ed.), *Public Opinion 1935-1946* (Princeton: Princeton University Press, 1951), p. 939.

[10] Leahy Diary, January 5, 1938, William D. Leahy Papers, Manuscript Division, Library of Congress. Cited hereafter as Leahy Papers. Roosevelt first proposed the increase in battleships and light cruisers as early as November 26, 1937, in a conference with Leahy. Leahy Diary, November 26, 1937, Leahy Papers.

[11] Newman, p. 252; see also Davis, p. 372.

[12] *New York Herald Tribune*, January 29, 1938, p. 1.

[13] Leahy Diary, January 28, 1938, Leahy Papers.

[14] *New York Times*, February 12, 1938, p. 1.

[15] Arthur A. Ekirch, Jr., *The Civilian and the Military* (New York: Oxford University Press, 1956), p. 249; See also U.S., Department of State, *Public Attitude Studies* (Washington: GPO, 1942), p. 20.

[16] *New York Herald Tribune*, January 29, 1938, p. 10; *Newark Evening News*, February 1, 1938, p. 12; *Baltimore Sun*, February 4, 1938, p. 12.

[17] *Birmingham News*, February 1, 1938, p. 6; *Cincinnati Inquirer*, January 29, 1938, p. 16; *Omaha World Herald*, January 29, 1938, p. 16; *Des Moines Register*, January 29, 1938, p 4; *Minneapolis Tribune*, January 29, 1938, p. 14; *Butte Standard* (Montana), January 30, 1938, p. 10; *Arizona Republic*, January 30, 1938, p. 10.

[18] *Christian Century*, 55 (February 23, 1938), 230-231; *Scholastic*, 32 (February 26, 1938), 2; *New Republic*, 94 (February 9, 1938), 17.

[19] *Literary Digest*, 125 (January 8, 1938), 4; (February 12, 1938), 4.

[20] *New York Times,* December 30, 1937, p. 18; *Boston Globe,* January 29, 1938, p. 12; *Providence Journal,* January 29, 1938, p. 10; *Philadelphia Inquirer,* January 29, 1938, p. 6.

[21] *Buffalo Evening News,* January 29, 1938, p. 4; *Pittsburgh Post-Gazette,* January 29, 1938, p. 8; *Cleveland Plain Dealer,* January 29, 1938, p. 4; *Detroit Free Press,* January 31, 1938, p. 6.

[22] *Richmond Times-Dispatch,* January 29, 1938, p. 6; *New Orleans Times-Picayune,* January 29, 1938, p. 8; *Nashville Banner,* February 3, 1938, p. 4.

[23] *Indianapolis Star,* January 29, 1938, p. 8; *St. Louis Post-Dispatch,* January 29, 1938, p. 4; *Chicago Tribune,* December 18, 1937, p. 12; *Chicago Daily News,* January 29, 1938, p. 14; *Milwaukee Journal,* January 29, 1938, p. 4.

[24] *Salt Lake City Tribune,* January 11, 1938, p. 8; *Albuquerque Journal,* January 29, 1938, p. 10; *Los Angeles Times,* December 30, 1937, p. 4; *Sacramento Union,* January 30, 1938, p. 6; *San Francisco Chronicle,* January 29, 1938, p. 10; *Portland Oregonian,* January 29, 1938, p. 10; *Seattle Daily Times,* January 30, 1938, p. 6; *Scientific American,* 159 (March, 1938), 137.

[25] *Los Angeles Times,* January 11, 1938, p. 11.

[26] *The Times* (London), January 29, 1938, p. 13; *The Economist* (London), 131 (February 5, 1938), 284; *London Observor,* February 13, 1938, p. 18.

[27] U.S., Department of State, *Documents on German Foreign Policy, 1918-1945,* Series D (Washington: GPO, 1949), I, 663.

[28] *New York Times,* February 3, 1938, p. 6.

[29] *Tokyo Asahi,* January 31, 1938, p. 8; *Japan Times and Mail,* February 4, 1938, p. 8; *Tokyo Nichi Nichi,* February 7, 1938, p. 8; *Miyako,* February 8, 1938, p. 7; *Tokyo Yoimuri,* February 10, 1938, p. 6.

[30] *Japan Times and Mail,* February 2, 1938, p. 1; *Ibid.,* February 8, 1938, p. 1; *New York Times,* February 28, 1938, p. 6.

[31] U.S., Department of State, *Peace and War, United States Foreign Policy, 1931-1941* (Washington: GPO, 1943), pp. 303-304. Cited hereafter as *Peace and War, 1931-1941.*

[32] *Japan Times and Mail,* February 7, 1938, p. 8.

[33] *Peace and War, 1931-1941,* p. 305.

[34] *Japan Times and Mail,* February 14, 1938, p. 1.

[35] Press Conference, February 15, 1938, OF 18, Roosevelt Papers.

[36] *Peace and War, 1931-1941,* pp. 306-307.

[37] U.S., Congress, House, *Debate on the Naval Bill,* 75th Cong., 3rd Sess., 1938, p. 3323.

[38] *Ibid.,* p. 3325; *Indianapolis Star,* January 9, 1938, p. 19.

[39] U.S., *Congressional Record,* 75th Cong., 3rd Sess., 1938, LXXXIII, Part 2, 593, 1012, 3503.

[40] *Ibid.,* 3417-3421.

[41] *Ibid.,* 809-810, 3433.

[42] *Ibid.,* 348.

[43] *Ibid.,* 3499-3500.

[44] *Ibid.,* 3522, 3532.

[45] U.S., Congress, House, Committee on Naval Affairs, *Hearings to Establish the Composition of the Navy,* 75th Cong., 3rd Sess., 1938, pp. 1984-1985. Cited hereafter as House Committee on Naval Affairs, *Naval Hearings,* 1938.

[46] *Ibid.,* pp. 1988-1990.

[47] *Congressional Digest,* 17 (March, 1938), 91.

[48] House Committee on Naval Affairs, *Naval Hearings,* 1938, p. 2241, 2873; Beard, pp. 216-217.

[49] U.S., *Congressional Record,* 75th Cong., 3rd Sess., 1938, LXXXIII, Part 2, 5780-5781.

[50] Correspondence, April 4, 1938, William E. Borah Papers, Manuscript Division, Library of Congress.

[51] U.S., *Congressional Record,* 75th Cong., 3rd Sess., 1938, LXXXIII, Part 2, 5903, 5610-5613.

[52] *Ibid.,* 689.

[53] *Ibid.,* 1622; Davis, p. 377.

[54] U.S., *Congressional Record,* 75th Cong., 3rd Sess., 1938, LXXXIII, Part 2, 6019, 1193-1194.

[55] *Ibid.,* 5517-5523, 6134.

[56] U.S., Congress, Senate, Committee on Naval Affairs, *Hearings, Naval Expansion Program,* 75th Cong., 3rd Sess., 1398, p. 59, 180, 221, 267.

[57] *Ibid.,* 214-215.

[58] *Ibid.,* 130.

[59] U.S., *Congressional Record,* 75th Cong., 3rd Sess., 1938, LXXXIII, Part 2, 6030, 5524.

[60] Neumann, pp. 250-251.

CHAPTER VI

SUMMARY

The *Panay* incident was the prelude to the eventual collapse of American-Japanese relations. Though most Americans in 1937 failed to comprehend its long-range effects, the attack upon the *Panay* was to serve notice of ominous events to come. Since the First World War, the United States had sought to uphold the status quo in Asia, but by the 1930's, Japan had largely upset the balance of power relationship there. After hostilities occurred between China and Japan in July, 1937, the American government was again confronted with some of the same difficult alternatives it had faced in 1931 over the Manchurian crisis. The United States government could continue its isolationist position and withdraw completely from China or it could intervene, directly or indirectly, in order to restrain the Japanese expansion in China. Both President Roosevelt and Secretary of State Hull felt that withdrawal from China would damage American economic, missionary, and philanthropic enterprises. Moreover, a withdrawal in the face of Japanese military pressure would injure American prestige abroad. Nor would the continuance of the Hoover-Stimson non-recognition policy, according to the President and his secretary of state, serve as an effective measure to end hostilities and re-establish the balance of power in the Far East. Applying an economic boycott by invoking the Third Neutrality Act against both belligerents also was distasteful to Roosevelt, who felt that the mandatory embargo would be more detrimental to China. Both men were well aware that any moves which pointed toward active intervention in the conflict would be disapproved by a predominantly isolationist Congress and by the public at large. Most Americans simply did not believe that the United States' stake in China was worth the risk of a possible war with Japan nor did they wish to embark again upon a crusade to make the world safe for democracy.

126

As a result of these various beliefs and pressures, the Roosevelt Administration adopted what was eventually a compromise plan. United States policy would henceforth be directed towards the maintenance of American rights and interests in China by means of diplomatic protests and by the actions of American diplomatic and consular officials on the spot. At the same time, the government would urge its nationals to evacuate the area of hostilities as quickly as possible. Indeed, the Administration made every effort to avoid any specific proposal which might result in the United States assuming the onus of leadership in any anti-Japanese movement.

Roosevelt still remained unconvinced, however, that such a formula would offer permanent protection for American nationals and interests in China. But the President was not able to devise any practicable arrangement that would ease the tension in the Far East. At best, moral pressure was brought to bear upon Japan to reach an amicable settlement with China. Such was the purpose of the Brussels Conference in November, 1937. Roosevelt remained ostensibly cautious in respect to taking a militant stand against Japan at the conference. A month earlier, he attempted to shift American diplomacy from its isolationist position, but the somewhat adverse reaction he received to his proposed quarantine plan made it apparent that the nation would oppose active intervention anywhere. None of the powers represented at the conference, as it turned out, was willing to go beyond censuring Japan for violating the Nine Power Treaty of 1922. Great Britain and France, in particular, considered the crisis in the Far East of secondary importance in comparison to the growing problems in Europe. They refused to become involved there unless the United States would cooperate actively. Such cooperation was not forthcoming. The Roosevelt Administration went no further than to re-affirm the American principles, as set forth by Hull on July 16, 1937, governing international relationships. The domestic reaction to Roosevelt's quarantine plan and the failure of the Brussels Conference helped to impress upon Japan that the United States would no more support intervention in the Far East, or elsewhere, in 1937 than it had in 1932 when the nation refused to support Stimson in his opposition to Japan's seizure of Manchuria.

These were the essential factors which influenced the American attitude when the Japanese bombed and sank the *Panay* in December, 1937. Generally in the past, such incidents would have resulted in some retaliatory measures by the United States. But the sinking of the *Panay* and its convoy aroused no nationwide outcry, no widespread demand in Congress or the press that the United States government avenge the incident by declaring war against Japan. It was quite evident that the anti-Japanese feeling in the United States was not intense enough to produce a pronounced drift towards war, especially when diplomatic consultations might be able to settle the issue. Hence, the general reaction in the United States was alarm, not that Japan would go unpunished, but that the *Panay* incident would involve the United States in an unwanted conflict. Only a few naval officials supported moves for an immediate showdown with Japan.

Both Roosevelt and Hull, at the outset, attempted to draw the Japanese Emperor into the political arena in an effort which they felt would restrain the Japanese militarists who had disregarded pledges made by civilian officials. At the same time, the President explored various ways to redeem American prestige in the Far East. Roosevelt even considered the possibility of freezing Japanese assets in the United States if negotiations proved unsuccessful. But beyond protesting diplomatically, neither he nor Hull had any intention of leading the nation into war over the crisis. The President fully realized that isolationist sentiment in the country would never tolerate, much less support, any armed intervention by the United States over the issue no matter what elements of prestige were called into play. One specific example of this sentiment was Louis Ludlow's proposed referendum on war. Through the resolution, many isolationists had sought to undermine the Executive's control of the nation's foreign policy. They also hoped that passage of the referendum would check any President from leading the country into an unpopular and unnecessary war. The referendum's defeat in January, 1938, by a narrow margin did indicate the strength of isolationist opinion in Congress. Though few Americans comprehended its significance, the defeat of the Ludlow Resolution marked the apex of pacifist influence during the 1930's in the United States.

The sinking of the *Panay* and the subsequent crisis it produced has precipitated an endless debate as to who had been directly responsible for the attack. The confusion attending the rapid Japanese advance upon Nanking, the reckless exuberence of victory, and the indifference of over-anxious pilots to the consequences which might result in an incident with a foreign power were probable background factors in the attack upon the vessel and its survivors. The immediate causes for the sinking, however, are somewhat confusing. At first glance it appeared that information regarding the gunboat's position had been withheld by Japanese army intelligence from the naval air squadron which had been requested to make the strike on December 12. Army intelligence merely informed the naval air units that Chinese soldiers were fleeing Nanking in four vessels but neglected to state the identity of the ships. The Japanese pilots approached their target certain that they were Chinese. The number of vessels, their location, and characteristics coincided with the description which had been supplied by the army. Writing about the event years later, Masatake Okumiya, one of the pilots involved in the attack, declared that the principal reasons for the Japanese failure to identify the target was a heavy reliance upon army reports and a desire for distinguished service in the Nanking campaign. Moreover, the pilots launched the attack hurriedly since they did not wish to give the enemy time enough to prepare for defensive action. Okumiya felt certain that the army did not attempt to dupe the navy intentionally into making an attack upon the American warship.[1]

Yet, further evidence indicated otherwise; that the attack upon the American convoy was anything but a question of mistaken identity. Since December 11, an almost hourly account had been dispatched to the Japanese military and civilian authorities, both in Shanghai and Tokyo announcing the changing positions of the *Panay* and its convoy. Even four hours prior to the attack, the gunboat's nationality was made known to a Japanese military unit which halted the vessel before it had reached its fateful rendezvous point 27 miles above Nanking. Film taken on December 12 by a cameraman on board the *Panay*, revealed a sunny and cloudless day and it also showed American flags painted and displayed prominently on each of the vessels.[2] It appears inconceivable that the Japanese pilots could have failed to identify the nationality of the vessels at such low altitudes. Nor did the Japanese fully explain the assault upon the gunboat by a motor launch following the initial aerial attack and the subsequent aerial machine-gunning of the vessel's survivors as they attempted to escape to shore. Indeed, both the Japanese Army and Navy endeavored to minimize any direct responsibility for the attack which explains the conflicting evidence reached in their respective investigations into the affair.

It appears doubtful that the Japanese government as a whole precipitated the incident. From their standpoint, the attack upon the American gunboat was nothing more than the result of mistaken identity. Throughout the Sino-Japanese conflict, the Japanese government maintained an astonishing lack of control over its forces in China, a fact which left certain high-ranking military officers somewhat free to determine the nation's military policies there. When the *Panay* episode ensued, the government was compelled to explain away the sinking to the United States government, and if need be, to bear the consequences which might possibly occur. The Japanese government made every effort to minimize the crisis and so avert any break in diplomatic relations. In 1937, Japan was still vitally dependent upon the United States for its raw materials and on the American market for its exports. Hence, when negotiations with the United States seemed to reach an impasse, the Japanese government accepted full responsibility for the sinking and promptly paid the indemnities requested. It is evident that an elite inner group of Japanese military extremists attempted to provoke a clash with the United States by attacking the *Panay*. At the very least, these radical elements hoped to pressure the Western democracies to withdraw from China completely.

After the affair had been settled, the President evinced some doubt as to whether the United States could rely upon Japan not to jeopardize American rights and interests again in the Far East. The fact that Japan had invited such risks made the idea of hostilities between the two countries almost plausible. This uncertainty led Roosevelt to consider the possibility of a two-ocean war in the foreseeable future. He was also aware that a stronger American Navy was imperative. Even as early as the fall of 1937, the President pointed out this need though he remained doubtful, following the reaction to his quarantine proposal, whether Congress would support any measures for increasing the navy. It was the effects of the *Panay* affair coupled with the reported information of Japanese naval expansion that provided the impetus Roosevelt needed to pursue a program of naval building in January, 1938. Though his naval plan was designated essentially as a defensive measure, the increases were intended specifically as a containment to the rising naval preponderance of Japan in the Pacific. Yet there was another more significant implication to the President's naval program. Roosevelt feared that the nation would remain aloof indefinitely from world problems. His rearmament program was merely one attempt to arouse a complacent nation to the impending dangers of fascism and aggression. The nation did not depart radically, however, from its passive nature following the passage of the naval bill; it refused to take the initiative until it had no other choice. Nor was American foreign policy substantially altered immediately following the *Panay* affair. The *Panay* incident simply reflected America's refusal to undertake a more positive program. Nevertheless, the episode had a significant impact upon future American diplomacy in the Far East since it served ultimately as a vital turning point in American-Japanese relations. For the Japanese, the *Panay* incident was an obvious way station en route to Pearl Harbor.

Notes

[1] Masatake Okumiya, "How The *Panay* Was Sunk," *United States Naval Institute Proceedings* 79, (June, 1953), 592-596.

[2] Universal Pictures Film No. 506, Motion Picture Division, National Archives.

APPENDIX I

Treaty Allowances Under The Washington Treaty of 1922 and the London Treaty of 1930[1]

Vessels	U.S. (15 vessels)	G.B. (15 vessels)	Japan (9 vessels)	France —	Italy —
1. capital ships	525,000	525,000	315,000	*175,000	*175,000
2. aircraft carriers	135,000	135,000	81,000	60,000	60,000
3. cruisers A (Heavy)	180,000	146,000	108,000	X	X
4. cruisers B (Light)	143,500	192,000	100,000	X	X
5. destroyers	150,000	150,000	105,500	X	X
6. submarines	52,700	52,700	52,700	X	X
Total tonnage	1,186,200	1,200,700	762,200	—	—

X France and Italy did not ratify the London Treaty of 1930 which had fixed the allowances in these categories.

* France and Italy were not limited as to the number of vessels but limited in tonnage to 175,000 T.

[1] U.S. *Congressional Record*, 75th Cong., 3rd Sess., 1938, LXXXIII, 5531.

APPENDIX II

Actual Tonnage and Ratios of Vessels Built, Being Built, and Appropriated For January 1, 1938[1]

	U.S.	G.B.	Japan	Ratio
1. capital ships	534,300	544,750	272,070	10:10.1:5.0
2. aircraft carriers	135,000	171,450	88,470	10:12.6:6.5
3. cruisers with over 6" guns	171,800	144,220	107,800	10:8.3:6.2
4. crusiers with 6" guns	160,500	336,870	135,525	10:20.9:8.4
5. destroyers	306,795	249,019	142,503	10:8.1:4.6
6. submarines	93,295	67,104	24,498	10:7.7:2.6
Total (tons)	1,401,690	1,513,413	770,866	10:10.7:5.4

APPENDIX III

Actual Tonnage and Ratios of Under-age Vessels (February 16, 1938)[2]

	U.S.	G.B.	Japan	Ratio
1. capital ships	464,300	474,750	272,070	10:10.2:5.8
2. aircraft carriers	100,400	115,350	68,370	10:11.2:6.8
3. cruisers with over 6" guns	161,200	144,220	107,800	10:8.9:6.6
4. cruisers with 6" guns	90,500	175,830	83,495	10:19.3:9.2
5. destroyers	74,780	118,654	102,933	10:15.7:13.6
6. submarines	34,025	47,319	59,512	10:13.8:17.5
Total (tons)	925,205	1,076,123	694,180	10:11.6:7.5

[1] U. S. *Congressional Record*, 75th Cong., 3rd Sess., 1938 LXXXIII, Part 2, 966.
[2] U. S. *Congressional Record*, 75th Cong., 3rd Sess., 1938 LXXXIII, Part 2, 966.

APPENDIX IV

U.S. Vessels Built, Being Built and Appropriated For as of March 15, 1938[1]

Type	Under-age Vessels According to 1936 London Treaty		Over-age Vessels According to 1936 London Treaty		TOTAL	
	No.	Approx. Tons				
1. capital ships	15	464,300	—	—	15	464,300
2. aircraft carriers	3	80,500	—	—	3	80,500
3. cruiser A	17	161,200	—	—	17	161,200
4. cruiser B	10	70,500	—	—	10	70,500
5. destroyers	35	53,080	168	190,260	203	243,340
6. submarines	22	32,580	62	43,340	84	75,920
TOTAL	102	862,160	230	233,600	332	1,095,760

Type	Being Built and Appropriated For		Grand Total	
1. capital ships	2	70,000	17	534,300
2. aircraft carriers	3	54,500	6	135,000
3. cruisers A	1	10,000	18	171,200
4. cruisers B	9	90,000	19	160,500
5. destroyers	49	76,050	252	319,390
6. submarines	16	23,185	100	99,105
TOTAL	80	323,735	412	1,419,495

[1] U. S. *Congressional Record*, 75th Cong., 3rd Sess., 1938 LXXXIII, Part 2, 5532.

APPENDIX V

Comparison of sizes of navies in the event Japan and G.B. build no additional naval vessels and the U.S. completes the naval vessels authorized by the second Vinson-Trammell Naval bill (May, 1938)[1]

	G.B.		U.S.		Japan		France	
Vessel	Tons	Ratio	Tons	Ratio	Tons	Ratio	Tons	Ratio
1. capital ships	7.3	5	7.1	4.9	4.2	2.9	2.3	1.6
2. aircraft carriers	2.5	5	1.6	3.2	1.4	2.8	.6	1.2
3. cruisers A	.4	4.1	1.7	5	.5	4.4	.7	2.1
4. cruisers B	4.5	5	2.4	2.7	2.2	2.4	1	1.1
5. destroyers	2.7	3.6	3.7	5	2.2	2.9	1.5	2
6. submarines	.8	3.3	1.2	5	.9	3.8	.9	3.8
TOTAL	18.2	5	17.7	4.6	11.4	3.2	7	1.8

	Italy		Germany		U.S.S.R.	
	Tons	Ratio	Tons	Ratio	Tons	Ratio
1. capital ships	2.3	1.6	2.1	1.4	1.7	1.2
2. aircraft carriers	0	0	.4	.8	.2	.4
3. cruisers A	.8	2.4	.3	.9	1.5	.4
4. cruisers B	.8	.9	.7	.8	.3	4.3
5. destroyers	1.6	2.2	.5	.68	.7	.95
6. submarines	1.1	4.6	.3	1.3	.9	3.8
TOTAL	6.6	1.7	4.3	1.1	5.3	1.1

---

[1] U. S. *Congressional Record*, 75th Cong., 3rd Sess., 1938 LXXXIII, Part 2, 5532.

APPENDIX VI

United States Naval Displacement[1]

Vessel	Original Treaty Allowance		Increases Due to Invoking "Escalator Clause," Art. 21 London Treaty (1936)
	No.	Tons	
1. capital ships	15	525,000	—
2. aircraft carriers	—	135,000	—
3. cruisers A	18	180,000	—
4. cruisers B	—	143,500	20,270
5. destroyers	—	150,000	40,000
6. submarines	—	52,700	15,598
TOTAL		1,186,200	75,868

Vessel	Total Authorized Under Vinson-Trammell Act (1934) Under-age Vessels		Authorized Under Second Vinson Bill (1938) Under-age Vessels	
1. capital ships	15	525,000	3	135,000
2. aircraft carriers	6	135,000	2	40,000
3. cruisers A	18	180,000	..	......
4. cruisers B	19	163,770	9	68,754
5. destroyers	121	190,000	23	38,000
6. submarines	47	68,298	9	13,658
TOTAL	227	1,262,068	46	295,412

Grand Total

Vessel		
1. capital ships	18	660,000
2. aircraft carriers	8	175,000
3. cruisers A	18	180,000
4. cruisers B	28	232,524
5. destroyers	144	228,000
6. submarines	56	81,956
TOTAL	272	1,557,480

[1] U. S. *Congressional Record*, 75th Cong., 3rd Sess., 1938 LXXXIII, Part 2, 5529.

BIBLIOGRAPHY

BIBLIOGRAPHICAL GUIDES:

Hamer, P. G. *A Guide to Archives and Manuscripts in the United States.* New Haven: Yale University Press, 1961.

Handlin, Oscar, et al. (eds.). *Harvard Guide to American History.* Cambridge: Harvard University Press, 1954.

Howe, George F. (ed.). *American Historical Association's Guide to Historical Literature.* New York: The Macmillan Co., 1961.

Plischke, Elmer. *American Foreign Relations: A Bibliography of Official Sources.* College Park: University of Maryland Press, 1955.

U. S. National Archives. *Guide to Materials in the National Archives.* Washington: GPO, 1948.

PRIMARY SOURCES:
Manuscripts and Unprinted Material:

Franklin D. Roosevelt Library, Hyde Park, New York
    Franklin D. Roosevelt Papers.
    R. Walton Moore Papers.

Lilly Library, Indiana University
    Louis Ludlow Papers.

Manuscript Division, Library of Congress
    William E. Borah Papers.
    Norman H. Davis Papers.
    Cordell Hull Papers.
    William D. Leahy Papers.
    Harry E. Yarnell Papers.

National Archives
    Historical Division, Department of State. Attitudes of Organized Pressure Groups, 1920-1945. (Typescript.)
    Historical Division, Department of State. Press Releases, December, 1937.
    Historical Division, Department of State. Diplomatic Records, Record Group 59.
    Legislative Division. Papers Accompanying Specific Bills and Resolutions.
    Legislative Division. Public Attitudes on the Ludlow Referendum, December, 1937-January, 1938. (Typescript.)
    Motion Pictures Division. "Bombing of the *USS Panay.*" Universal Pictures Film No. 506.
    Motion Pictures Division. "The Battle of China." United States Signal Corps Orientation Film No. 6.
    Naval History Division. Correspondence Relating to the Sinking of the *USS Panay.* Record Group 45.
    Naval History Division. Press Releases, December, 1937.

United States Government Documents:

Congressional Record, 75th Cong., 2nd Sess., 1937, LXXXII.

Congressional Record, 75th Cong., 3rd Sess., 1938, LXXXIII.

Department of the Army. Office of Chief of Military History. *Japanese Monographs No. 144, China Area Operations Record.* Washington: GPO, 1957.

Department of State. *The Conference of Brussels, November 3-24, 1937.* Washington: GPO, 1938.

Department of State. *Documents on German Foreign Policy, 1918-1945.* Series D, Vol. 1. Washington: GPO, 1949.

Department of State. *Foreign Relations of the United States, Diplomatic Papers, 1937.* Vols. III, IV. Washington: GPO, 1954.

Department of State. *Foreign Relations of the United States, Japan, 1931-1941.* Washington: GPO, 1943.

Department of State. *Peace and War: United States Foreign Policy, 1931-1941.* Washington: GPO, 1943.

Department of State. *Public Attitude Studies.* Washington: GPO, 1941.

House of Representatives, Committee on Foreign Affairs. *Report on Sinking of United States Gunboat Panay.* 75th Cong., 2nd Sess., 1937.

House of Representatives, Committee on Naval Affairs. *Hearings to Establish the Composition of the Navy.* 75th Cong., 3rd Sess., 1938.

House of Representatives. *Debate on the Naval Bill.* 75th Cong., 3rd Sess., 1938.

House of Representatives. *Hearings on Ludlow Referendum on Participation in Foreign Wars.* 75th Cong., 2nd Sess., 1937.

House of Representatives. *Hearings on Proposed Withdrawal of United States Gunboats in China.* 75th Cong., 3rd Sess., 1938.

House of Representatives. *Hearings on Sinking of United States Gunboat Panay.* 75th Cong., 2nd Sess., 1937.

House of Representatives. *Report of the Secretary of State Relative to American Nationals, Armed Forces, and Investments in China.* 75th Cong., 3rd Sess., 1938.

Senate, Committee on Naval Affairs. *Hearings, Naval Expansion Program.* 75th Cong., 3rd Sess., 1938.

Senate. *Debate on the Naval Bill,* 75th Cong., 3rd Sess., 1938.

Senate. *Hearings on Sinking of United States Gunboat Panay.* 75th Cong., 2nd Sess., 1937.

Senate. *Resolution of Inquiry Relative to American Nationals, Armed Forces, and Investments in China.* 75th Cong., 3rd. Sess., 1938.

Other Printed Material:

Council on Foreign Relations. *Documents on American Foreign Relations, 1938-1939.* Vol. I. New York: Harper and Bros., 1940.

International Military Tribunal for the Far East. *Tokyo Trials: Proceedings of the Military Tribunal for the Far East.* Tokyo: Court House of the Tribunal War Ministry Bldg., 1946-1948.

Jones, S. Shepard and Denys P. Meyers. *Documents on American Foreign Relations.* Vol. 1. Boston: World Peace Foundation, 1939.

Roosevelt, Elliott (ed.). *F.D.R. His Personal Letters, 1928-1945.* Vol. I, II. New York: Duell, Sloan and Pearce, 1950.

Rosenman, Samuel I. (ed.). *The Public Papers and Addresses of Franklin D. Roosevelt.* Vols. VI, VII. New York: The MacMillan Co., 1941.

Newspapers:

(December 1937-March 1938 unless indicated otherwise.)
Albuquerque Journal
Arizona Republic
Atlanta Journal
Baltimore Sun
Birmingham News
Boston Globe
Buffalo Evening News
Butte Standard (Montana)
Charleston News and Courier (South Carolina)
Chicago Daily News
Chicago Tribune
Christian Science Monitor
Cincinnati Inquirer
Cleveland Plain Dealer
Dallas Morning News
Des Moines Register
Detroit Free Press
Echo de Paris, December, 1937.
Indianapolis Star
Japan Times and Mail
London Observor
Los Angeles Times
Louisville Times
Manchester Guardian
Milwaukee Journal
Minneapolis Daily Tribune
Miyako (Tokyo)
Montreal Daily Star, December, 1937.
Montreal Gazette, December, 1937.
Nashville Banner
Newark Evening News
New Orleans Times-Picayune
New York Daily Worker
New York Herald Tribune
New York Times, December 1937-May, 1938.
Omaha World Herald
Ottawa Journal, December, 1937.
Paris Je Suis Partout, December, 1937.
Paris L'Action Francaise, December, 1937.
Paris La Croix, December, 1937.
Paris Le Temps, December, 1937.
Philadelphia Inquirer
Pittsburgh Post-Gazette
Portland Oregonian
Providence Journal
Regina Leader Post, December, 1937.
Richmond Times-Dispatch
Rocky Mountain News
Sacramento Union
Salt Lake City Tribune
San Francisco Chronicle
Seattle Daily Times
St. Louis Post-Dispatch
The Times (London)

Tokyo Asahi
Tokyo Kokumin, December, 1937.
Tokyo Nichi Nichi
Tokyo Yoimuri
Toronto Globe and Mail, December, 1937.
Washington Evening Star
Washington Post
Welland Tribune, December, 1937.
Winnipeg Free Press, December, 1937.
Winnipeg Tribune, December, 1937.

Periodicals:

Alley, Norman, "Jim Felt Lucky," *Colliers,* 101 (February 12, 1938).

"America Accepts Japan's Apologies for the Sinking of the *USS Panay* but Issues Stern Warning." *China Weekly Review,* 83 (January 1, 1938).

"America Papers Echo Resentment of People over Bombing of *Panay.*" *China Weekly Review,* 83 (January 15, 1938).

China Quarterly, 3 (Summer 1938).

Congressional Digest, 17 (February-March 1938).

Current History and Forum, 47 (October 1937).

Dennett, Tyler. "Alternative American Policies in the Far East." *Foreign Affairs,* 16 (April 1938).

Flynn, J. T. "Landon-Roosevelt War-Game Huddle," *New Republic,* 93 (December 1937).

Fortune, 17 (March 1938).

"From *Lusitania* to *Panay,*" *New Republic,* 93 (December 1937).

Gallup, George and Claude Robinson. "America Public Opinion Survey, 1935-1938." *Public Opinion Quarterly,* 2 (July 1938).

"Great Mistake," *Time,* 30 (December 20, 1937).

Herring, Hubert. "Where Are You Going, Mr. President?" *Harpers,* 177 (May 1938).

Homan, Paul T. "Must It Be War With Japan?" *Political Science Quarterly,* 53 (June 1938).

Knox, Dudley W. "Peace and the Navy," *The Atlantic Monthly,* 161 (April 1938).

"Le Drame du *Panay,*" *Illustration,* 199 (January 15, 1938).

Life, 3 (December 1938).

Moley, Raymond. "Appeal to Heaven," *Newsweek,* 10 (December 27, 1937).

National Education Association Journal, 26 (December 1937).

Nelson, Carl J. "American Attitudes Toward Japan and China, 1937-1938." *Public Opinion Quarterly,* 3 (January 1939).

"*Panay* Backwash," *Literary Digest,* 125 (January 1, 1938).

"*Panay* Bill more that Two Million Dollars," *China Weekly Review,* 84 (April 2, 1939).

"*Panay* Bombed and Sunk," *Literary Digest,* 124 (December 25, 1937).

"*Panay* Incident Closed?" *Literary Digest,* 125 (January 8, 1938).

"*Panay* Pandomonium," *Time,* 30 (December 27, 1937).

"*Panay* Repercussions," *Time,* 31 (January 3, 1938).

"Photographs," *Newsweek,* 11 (January 17, 1938).

Popper, David H. "*Panay*—A Test of U. S. Foreign Policy," *Foreign Policy Bulletin,* 17 (December 24, 1937).

——————————. "U. S. Takes Firm Stand on *Panay* Incident," *Foreign Policy Bulletin,* 17 (December 17, 1937).

Scientific American, 159 (March 1938).

"Sinking of a Gunboat Changes Aspects of China War," *Newsweek*, 10 (December 27, 1938).

"Sinking of the *Panay*," *Christian Century*, 54 (December 22, 1937).

"Sinking of *Panay* Stiffens U. S. Anti-Japanese Stand," *Scholastic*, 31 (January 8, 1938).

Survey of International Affairs, 3 (January 1938).

"Survivors from *USS Panay* Confirm that Japanese Army Units Machine Gunned Ill-Fated Warship," *China Weekly Review*, 83 (December 25, 1937).

Takaishi, Shingoro. "Japan-American Friendship," *Contemporary Japan*, 7 (January 1938).

The Economist (London), 131 (January-March 1938).

SECONDARY SOURCES:

Books:

Adler, Selig. *Isolationist Impulse: Its Twentieth Century Reaction*. New York: Collier Books, 1961.

Allen, H. C. *Great Britain and the United States*. New York: St. Martin's Press, Inc., 1955.

America's Share is Japan's War Guilt. New York: American Committee for Non-Participation in Japanese Aggression, 1938.

Bailey, Thomas A. *A Diplomatic History of the American People*. 6th Ed. New York: Appleton-Century-Crofts Co., 1958.

——————————. *The Man in the Street: Impact of American Public Opinion on Foreign Policy*. New York: Macmillan Co., 1948.

Barnes, Harry E. (ed.) *Perpetual War for Perpetual Peace: A Critical Examination of the Foreign Policy of Franklin D. Roosevelt and Its Aftermath*. Caldwell: Caxton Printers Ltd., 1953.

Bartlett, Ruhl J. (ed.). *The Record of American Diplomacy: Documents and Readings in the History of American Foreign Relations*. New York: Alfred A. Knopf, 1964.

Beard, Charles A. *American Foreign Policy in the Making, 1932-1940: A Study in Responsibilities*. New Haven: Yale University Press, 1946.

Beckmann, George M. *The Modernization of China and Japan*. New York: Harper and Row, 1962.

Bemis, Samuel F. *A Short History of American Foreign Policy and Diplomacy*. New York: Henry Holt and Co., 1959.

——————————. *The United States as a World Power*. New York: Henry Holt and Co., 1950.

Bisson, T. A. *American Policy in the Far East, 1931-1940*. New York: Institute of Pacific Relations, Inquiry Series, 1940.

Bloch, Kurt. *German Interests and Policies in the Far East*. New York: Institute of Pacific Relations, 1939.

Blum, John Morton. *From the Morgenthau Diaries: Years of Crises 1928-1938*. Boston: Houghton Mifflin Co., 1959.

Borg, Dorothy. *The United States and the Far Eastern Crisis of 1933-1938*. Cambridge: Harvard University Press, 1964.

Borton, Hugh. *Japan Since 1931*. New York: Institute of Pacific Relations, 1940.

Browder, Earl. *Fighting For Peace*. New York: International Publishers Co., 1939.

Buell, Raymond L. *Isolated America*. New York: Alfred A. Knopf, Inc., 1940.

——————————. *The Washington Conference*. New York: D. Appleton and Co., 1922.

Burns, James M. *Roosevelt: The Lion and the Fox.* New York: Harcourt, Brace and Co., 1956.

Butow, Robert J. C. *Tojo and the Coming of the War.* Princeton: Princeton University Press, 1961.

Cantril, Hadley. (ed.). *Public Opinion 1935-1946.* Princeton: Princeton University Press, 1951.

Chamberlin, William H. *Japan Over Asia.* Boston: Little, Brown and Co., 1941.

Cole, Wayne S. *Senator Gerald P. Nye and American Foreign Relations.* Minneapolis: The University of Minnesota Press, 1962.

Craigie, Robert L. *Behind the Japanese Mask.* London: Hutchinson Ltd., 1940.

Credner, Wilhelm. *Japan und Die Vereinigten im Pazifischen Raum.* Jena: G. Fischer Ltd., 1940.

Current, Richard N. *Secretary Stimson: A Study In Statescraft.* New Brunswick: Rutgers University Press, 1954.

Davids, S. Jules. *America and the World of Our Time: United States Diplomacy in the Twentieth Century.* New York: Random House, 1960.

Davis, George T. *A Navy Second to None.* New York: Harcourt, Brace and Co., 1940.

De Conde, Alexander. *A History of American Foreign Policy.* New York: Charles Scribner's Sons, 1963.

——————————. (ed.). *Isolation and Security.* Durham: Duke University Press, 1957.

Divine, Robert A. *The Illusion of Neutrality.* Chicago: The University of Chicago Press, 1962.

——————————. *The Reluctant Belligerent: American Entry Into World War II.* New York: John Wiley and Sons, Inc., 1965.

Drummond, Donald F. *The Passing of American Neutrality, 1937-1941.* Ann Arbor: University of Michigan Press, 1955.

Dulles, Foster R. *China and America.* Princeton: Princeton University Press, 1946.

Duroselle, Jean-Baptiste. *De Wilson à Roosevelt: Politique Exterieure des Etats-Unis, 1913-1945.* Paris: Librairie, Armand Colin, 1960.

Ekirch, Arthur A., Jr. *The Civilian and the Military.* New York: Oxford University Press, 1956.

Fairbank, John K. *The United States and China.* Cambridge: Harvard University Press, 1958.

Falk, Edwin A. *From Perry to Pearl Harbor.* Garden City: Doubleday, Doran and Co., Inc., 1943.

Farley, James A. *Jim Farley's Story: The Roosevelt Years.* New York: Whittlesey House, McGraw-Hill Book Co., Inc., 1948.

Feis, Herbert. *The Road to Pearl Harbor.* Princeton: Princeton University Press, 1950.

Friedman, Irving S. *British Relations With China: 1931-1939.* New York: Institute of Pacific Relations, 1940.

Fry, Varian. *War In China: America's Role in the Far East.* New York: Foreign Policy Assn., 1938.

Gallup, George, and Saul F. Rae. *The Pulse of Democracy.* New York: Simon and Schuster Inc., 1940.

Gayer, Arthur D., and Carl T. Schmidt. *American Economic Foreign Policy.* New York: American Coordinating Committee for International Studies, 1939.

Graebner, Norman A. *An Uncertain Tradition: American Secretaries of State in the Twentieth Century.* New York: McGraw-Hill Book Co., Inc., 1961.

Grew, Joseph C. *Ten Years In Japan.* New York: Simon and Schuster, Inc., 1944.

—————————. *Turbulent Era*. Vol. II. Boston: Houghton Mifflin Co., 1952.

Grigg, Richard. *Japanese-American Relations, 1931-1937*. Washington: GPO, 1950.

Griswold, A. W. *Far-Eastern Policy of the United States*. New York: Harcourt Brace and Co., 1938.

Halasz, Nicholas. *Roosevelt Through Foreign Eyes*. Princeton: D. Van Nostrand Co., Inc., 1961.

Hanson, Haldore. *Humane Endeavor: The Story of the China War*. New York: Farrar and Rinehart Inc., 1939.

Hartmann, Frederick H. *The Relations of Nations*. New York: The Macmillan Co., 1957.

Hinton, Harold B. *Cordell Hull: A Biography*. Garden City. Doubleday, Doran and Co., Inc., 1942.

Hooker, Nancy H. (ed.). *The Moffat Papers: Selections from the Diplomatic Journals of Jay Pierrepont Moffat, 1919-1943*. Cambridge: Harvard University Press, 1956.

Hornbeck, Stanley K. *The United States and the Far East: Certain Fundamentals of Policy*. Boston: World Peace Foundation, 1942.

Hsu, Shuhsi. *Japan and the Third Powers*. Shanghai: Kelly and Walsh Ltd., 1941.

Hudson, G. F. *The Far East in World Politics*. New York: Oxford University Press, 1939.

Hull, Cordell. *The Memoirs of Cordell Hull*. Vol. I. New York: The Macmillan Co., 1948.

Ickes, Harold L. *The Secret Diary of Harold L. Ickes*. Vol. II. New York: Simon and Schuster Inc., 1954.

Johnson, Walter. *1600 Pennsylvania Avenue*. Boston: Little, Brown and Co., 1960.

Johnstone, William C. *The United States and Japan's New Order*. New York: Oxford University Press, 1941.

Jones, Francis C. *Japan's New Order in East Asia: Its Rise and Fall, 1937-1945*. London: Oxford University Press, 1954.

Knox, Dudley W. *A History of the United States Navy*. New York: G. P. Putnam's Sons, 1948.

Langer, William L., and S. Everett Gleason. *The Challenge to Isolation, 1937-1940*. New York: Harper and Bros., 1952.

Latane, John H. *A History of American Foreign Policy, 1776-1940*. New York: Doubleday, Doran and Co., 1941.

Leahy, William. *I Was There*. New York: Whittlesey House, McGraw-Hill Book Co., Inc., 1950.

Leopold, R. W. *The Growth of American Foreign Policy: A History*. New York: Alfred A. Knopf Inc., 1962.

Levy, Roger. *French Interests and Policies in the Far East*. New York: Institute of Pacific Relations, 1941.

Lockwood, William W. (ed.). *Our Far Eastern Record*. Vol. I. New York: Institute of Pacific Relations, 1940.

Lory, Hillis. *Japan's Military Masters*. New York: The Viking Press, 1947.

McKenna, Marian C. *Borah*. Ann Arbor: The University of Michigan Press, 1961.

Max, Alfred. *Politique Exteriuere des Etats-Unis*. Paris: Hartmann Ltd., 1939.

Maxon, Yale C. *Control of Japanese Foreign Policy: A Study of Civil-Military Rivalry, 1930-1945*. Berkeley: University of California Press, 1957.

Millis, Walter. *Arms and the State*. New York: Twentieh Century Fund, 1958.

Mitchell, Donald W. *History of the Modern American Navy*. New York: Alfred A. Knopf Inc., 1946.

Moore, Frederick. *With Japan's Leaders: An Intimate Record of Fourteen Years as Counsellor to the Japanese, Ending December 7, 1941.* New York: Charles Scribner's Sons, 1942.

Moore, Harriet L. *Soviet Far Eastern Policy, 1931-1945.* Princeton: Princeton University Press, 1945.

Morison, Elting E. *Turmoil and Tradition: A Study of the Life and Times of Henry L. Stimson.* Boston: Houghton Mifflin Co., 1960.

Morison, Samuel E. *The Rising Sun In the Pacific, 1931-April 1942,* Vol. III; *History of the United States Naval Operations in World War II.* Boston: Little, Brown and Co., 1955.

Neumann, William L. *America Encounters Japan: From Perry to MacArthur.* Baltimore: Johns Hopkins Press, 1963.

Nevins, Allen. *The New Deal and World Affairs: A Chronicle of International Affairs, 1933-1945.* New Haven: Yale University Press, 1950.

O'Connor, Raymond G. *Perilous Equilibrium: The United States and the London Naval Conference of 1930.* Lawrence: University of Kansas Press, 1962.

Oliver, Frank. *Special Undeclared War.* London: Jonathan Cape Ltd., 1939.

Osgood, Robert E. *Ideals and Self-Interest in America's Foreign Relations.* Chicago: University of Chicago Press, 1953.

Perkins, Dexter. *The New Age of Franklin Roosevelt, 1932-1945.* Chicago: University of Chicago Press, 1957.

Pratt, Julius W. *A History of United States Foreign Policy.* Englewood: Prentice-Hall, Inc., 1961.

Quigley, Harold S. *Far Eastern War, 1937-1941.* Boston: Little Brown and Co. 1942.

Sanborn, Frederick R. *Design For War: A Study of Secret Power Politics, 1937-1941.* New York: The Devin-Adair Co., 1951.

Schroeder, Paul W. *The Axis Alliance and Japanese-American Relations, 1941.* Ithaca: Cornell University Press, 1958.

Smith, Robert A. *Our Future In Asia.* New York: The Viking Press, 1940.
——————. *Your Foreign Policy: How What and Why.* New York: The Viking Press, 1941.

Sprout, Harold and Margaret. *Toward a New Order of Sea Power.* Princeton: Princeton University Press, 1940.

Storry, Richard. *A History of Modern Japan.* Baltimore: Penquin Books Inc., 1960.
——————. *The Double Patriots: A Study of Japanese Nationalism.* London: Chatto and Windus Ltd., 1957.

Tansill, Charles C. *Back Door to War: The Roosevelt Foreign Policy, 1933-1941.* Chicago: Henry Regnery Co., 1952.

Tarasaki, Hidenari. *Bridge to the Sun.* Chapel Hill: The University of North Carolina Press, 1957.

Toynbee, Arnold J. *Survey of International Affairs.* Vol. I. London: Oxford University Press, 1941.

Tugwell, Rexford G. *The Democratic Roosevelt.* Garden City: Doubleday and Co., Inc., 1957.

Tupper, Eleanor and George E. McReynolds. *Japan in American Public Opinion.* New York: The Macmillan Co., 1937.

Van Alstyne, Richard W. *American Diplomacy in Action.* Stanford: Stanford University Press, 1944.

Vinacke, Harold M. *A History of the Far East in Modern Times.* New York: Appleton-Century-Crofts Co., 1959.

Wescott, Allan F. (ed.). *American Seapower Since 1775.* Chicago: J. B. Lippincott Co., 1947.

Yanaga, Chitoshi. *Japan Since Perry*. New York: McGraw-Hill Book Co., Inc., 1949.
Yoshihashi, Takehiko. *Conspiracy at Mukden: The Rise of the Japanese Military*. New Haven: Yale University Press, 1963.

Contemporary Articles:

Bolles, Blair. "Roosevelt's Foreign Policy," *Foreign Policy Reports,* 24 (August 1, 1945).
Gale, Esson M. "Yangtze Patrol," *United States Naval Institute Proceedings,* 81 (March 1955).
Okumiya, Masatake. "How The Panay Was Sunk," *United States Naval Institute Proceedings,* 79 (June 1953).
Tolley, Kemp. "Yang-Pat-Shanghai To Chunking," *United States Naval Institute Proceedings,* 89 (June 1963).

INDEX

This book was set in Linotype Baskerville, with chapter headings in Tempo. Photographs are reproduced by permission from the National Archives and the U.S. Naval Photographic Center, Washington, D.C. The book was printed on 60 lb. Warren's Old Style stock at C. E. Pauley and Co., Indianapolis, Indiana, and bound by Heckman Bindery, North Manchester, Indiana. The jacket was designed by Al Gowan, Department of Creative Arts, Purdue, and printed by offset lithography by Krieger-Ragsdale & Company, Evansville, Indiana. Editorial and production work were supervised by Mrs. Eleanor Crandall, Assistant University Editor, Purdue.